Managerialism in the Public Sector
Perspectives and Prospects

Andrea Tomo

# Managerialism in the Public Sector Perspectives and Prospects

First published 2018
by Routledge

2 Park Square, Milton Park, Abingdon, Oxfordshire OX14 4RN
52 Vanderbilt Avenue, New York, NY 10017

*Routledge is an imprint of the Taylor & Francis Group, an informa business*

First issued in paperback 2020

British Library Cataloguing-in-Publication Data
A catalogue record for this book is available from the British Library

ISBN: 978-88-921-1342-8 (hbk-G. Giappichelli Editore)
ISBN: 978-1-138-31334-7 (hbk)
ISBN: 978-0-367-59050-5 (pbk)

Typeset in Simoncini Garamond
by G. Giappichelli Editore, Turin, Italy

*The manuscript has been subjected to the double blind peer review process prior to publication.*

*The manuscript has been funded by the Department of Economics Management Institutions, University of Naples "Federico II".*

# CONTENTS

# LIST OF FIGURES AND TABLES

**Figures**

**Tables**

**Boxes**

# ACKNOWLEDGMENTS

I wish to thank all the professors and colleagues of the Department of Economics, Management, Institutions, University of Naples "Federico II", especially those of the Organization Studies group, and above all Gianluigi Mangia and Riccardo Mercurio.

I would also thank my wife and colleague Rosanna, for her suggestions and feedbacks in our discussions, and my parents and sister for their support.

# INTRODUCTION

The purpose of this book is to offer insights into the complex and often unclear context of public sector management, providing a newer theoretical and practical approach to the analysis and interpretation of these issues. The book is grounded in the awareness that the public sector has too often shown inefficiencies, despite the bloody expensive measures that have been undertaken, and from manifold perspectives such as the economic, social, organizational, and institutional ones, among others.

Behind the failures of public sector management, it is possible to recognize classic bureaucratic problems, in spite of actions at multiple levels, and from both theoretical and practical perspectives, to search for solutions.

The current economic environment, characterized by high dynamism, has led private-sector companies to continually search for flexibility and adaptation to react to constant change. However, the increasing flexibility of the private sector has not been matched by an equal flexibility within the public sector. One good example, from recent years, is the strong push to digitization and innovation in regard to information exchange (e.g., electronic communications and documentation between businesses or individuals and public offices). In spite of these directives, public entities are themselves sometimes noncompliant, lacking integrated databases among different public administrations and failing to digitize legacy documents. The result of this imbalance in the public-private relationship is that private citizens and businesses express discomfort and frustration when coming into contact with the public sector.

The examples above are symptomatic of the lack of consideration by public agencies of the complexity that characterizes the social economic environment to date. Literature (e.g., Klijn, 2008; Meek, 2010) has been repeatedly acknowledged these limitations, especially emphasizing that public systems are still strongly anchored to an ancient tradition of bureaucratic, standardized, and repeated activities characterized by high rationality (Meek, 2010). Indeed, as well known from Simon's studies (1956), it is impossible to consider the existence of a perfect rationality, which means that rational behavior, even in the public sector, should be considered more as an exception than the rule (Klijn, 2008).

Understanding and explaining change and complex dynamics within specific contexts – including the public sector – represents a key concern in much of the literature on governance, and consequently exploring and assessing possible points of contact between studies of public administration and theories of complexity becomes paramount.

Several authors have addressed the theme of complexity in the public context. For instance, Klijn (2008) discussed complexity theories by considering that complexity in the public system is mainly linked to the transition from "government" to "governance," and to the increasingly central role played by networks in the public sector. Klijn (2008) also emphasized the importance of complexity theory in the understanding of change within systems and the dynamics that result from complex interactions among the actors involved.

Complexity theory has grown in importance over the last decade, and its development has enabled a universal method of practice that proposes a pragmatic and humanistic management practice. The application of complexity theory highlights the importance of the development of an organization's culture and communication, enabling it to be dynamic while maintaining coherence and stability. Such a culture places the workers, their values, and their mission at the heart of the organization's practices, recognizing that information technology may provide a framework for complex communication and knowledge use but cannot replace highly developed professional negotiations and cooperation.

Over the last twenty years, some steps in this direction have been made with the models of New Public Management (Hood, 1991) and New Public Governance (Kooiman and Jentoft, 2009; Osborne 2010a, 2010b), which have reflected going towards a "corporatization" of public administrations that should have met the above-mentioned criteria of efficiency and effectiveness.

Yet, this process does not seem to be completed, and in the majority of cases has been hardly slower than expected. In brief, some negative aspects that emerged in the literature during the 1950s and 1960s, referring to old-fashioned bureaucracy, are for certain still valid today, e.g., the "displacement of goals" (Merton, 1940) and the "work to rule" (Blau, 1955). The complexity of the public service world, in fact, limits the usefulness of classical and rational scientific management approaches like New Public Managerialism (NPM); its rigid application of performance management and strategic management is dysfunctional in the public context. The excessive focus on the optimization of results has led to an infrequent (or totally absent) consideration of the social, institutional, and economic factors (determining the context) that instead should be considered in imagining a better functioning and accountable public administration.

Indeed, too many issues remain unsolved. The reference is, above all, to performance measurement themes, historically affected by long-settled problems. Among these are questions relating to the "work to rule" (Blau, 1955) and the "displacement of goals" (Merton, 1940), not to mention the obsessive focus on rules and procedures, leading to proceduralization rather than fostering substantive change. Given the persistence of old bureaucratic logic that still permeates modern public administration, the path toward broad improvement in the quality of public services for stakeholders is still beyond reach.

Considering the social and public functions they are in charge of, public agencies must ensure that their work is oriented to search for the best administrative efficiency and effectiveness, and that this, in turn, is aimed at satisfying the public stakeholders. Furthermore, the previously highlighted (and still unsolved) issues indicate that effective change in the public sector is required. The theme of change in public administration is, in fact, one of the most recently debated topics, especially with reference to the need to abandon the excessive focus on rules/procedures, and rather move toward models that consider individuals and their behaviors as the core of the organization and of its dynamics. This approach now goes under the name of the "behavioral approach" (Hinna et al., 2016).

Therefore, in this study, issues related to complexity and contingencies are applied to the field of public administration, also taking into account the main theories in the organizational and management fields for analyzing the role of the context and forces that shape organizational boundaries and organizations' way of acting and behaving.

The book balances a theoretical and methodological approach with an empirical case, by providing two theoretical chapters followed by an empirical analysis of the Italian public sector.

On the basis of all the above, this book aims to answer the following research questions.

✓ *Which organizational features characterize modern public administration?*

✓ *What factors influence the predominance of different models? What aspects characterize the activities carried out by public servants?*

To do so, the book is divided into three chapters, of which the first and the second allow us to map the territory depicting the issues relating to the public sector management in theory and practice, while the third one offers an empirical assessment of the above-cited themes.

Chapter 1 analyzes the characteristics of classic bureaucracies to highlight their typical characteristics, implications, and limits, along with a specific focus on the historic lack of attention paid to the issues of complexity that are intrinsic to the public sector but often neglected. Then, relying upon a systematic literature review, the chapter aims to understand how studies in the wake of NPM have addressed and problematized post-bureaucratic models of public organizations. In doing so, it provides a state-of-art analysis of bureaucratic and post-bureaucratic models.

The review also aims to detect what the literature suggests in terms of possible viable solutions to the critical aspects of the old bureaucracy. The literature offers interesting insights concerning still-neglected issues that need to be deepened. First, there is a lack of attention toward individuals and their behaviors within public organizations. Additionally, greater attention has been paid to Anglo-Saxon countries, while Continental European countries – especially those in the Southern area – are still under-investigated despite their peculiarities.

Chapter 2 problematizes public-sector management through the perspective of the behavioral approach, regarding individuals and their behaviors as key to analyzing and interpreting the whole picture. First, the chapter addresses the debate on the behavioral approach and its importance, building on studies grounded in the for-profit sector, with a specific focus on the framework proposed by Huse (2007). Then the chapter deepens these issues by showing the main implications for the public sector. Literature review using the ISI Web of Knowledge research engine will deepen the issue of individual behaviors within the public sector. Findings will help to support and adapt the framework advanced by Huse (2007), identifying a specific framework to analyze and understand individual behaviors within public administrations. The last section of the chapter provides a discussion on how to locate the behavioral approach within the studies on the public sector, taking as a starting point a study by Geddes (2012) that provided an interesting review of the previous organizational models of public administration: Public Administration, New Public Management (NPM), and Collaborative Public Management (CPM). The discussion will be built on eleven management dimensions: Performance, Accountability, Community engagement, Values, Leadership, Employment relations, Management tasks, Decision-making, Structure, Processes, and Change.

The issues emerging from the first two chapters form the conceptual bases for the empirical analysis in Chapter 3. It aims to examine which organizational features characterize modern public administrations, what factors influence the predominance of different models, and what aspects characterize the activities carried out by public servants, because the literature has often highlighted contrasting results from the implementation of NPM reforms.

Thus, the chapter relies upon an analysis carried out in the Italian context, on the ground of its peculiar political, cultural, and contextual aspects. The analysis relies upon a mixed-method approach to better catch the nuances emerging from face-to-face interviews with participants after their completion of a questionnaire. The questionnaire, administered to 156 public employees, officers, and managers, allowed us to gather data on the degree of specialization of tasks (both horizontal and vertical), the degree of formalization of the tasks, motivation, managerial styles, organizational climate, and areas involving conflict. In addition, face-to-face interviews made it possible to better understand participants' proposals for solving the main issues regarding the public sector. Data from the questionnaires have been analyzed with Pearson's correlation test and linear regression analysis.

The descriptive statistics provide information that enables the discussion on which features characterize the activities that Italian public servants carry out, in terms of degrees of specialization, formalization, and motivation, as well as information on managerial styles and the organizational climate within participants' public agencies.

The correlation test aims to understand which relationships might exist between age, horizontal specialization degree, vertical specialization degree, formalization degree, personal motivation, conflict degree, job qualification, public administration of affiliation, public administration's priority, managerial styles, and solutions to improve motivation. Additionally, the test enhances the discussion on which features characterize the organizational models of the modern public administrations in Italy.

The linear regression was performed to test the dependence of personal motivation on the degrees of specialization, complexity, formalization, and conflict, and the managerial style. The results advance the understanding of which features influence public servants' motivation in carrying out their activities, because the literature highlights that low motivation is associated with high degrees of standardization and formalization.

The concluding chapter provides final remarks based on the analysis. Findings reveal that several issues regarding the public sector remain unsolved, despite several attempts made both theoretically and practically in searching for solutions to problems related to the old bureaucratic approach. The behavioral approach, by focusing on individuals and their behaviors, might provide responses to the highlighted problems. This approach, by putting individuals at the center of the analysis, advances the debate on public-sector issues. Finally, the statistical analysis carried out in Chapter 3 provides insights about the Italian setting, highlighting that the Italian public sector is still characterized by features of the old bureaucratic model and that, rather than being accompanied by post-bureaucratic revolutions, it is accompanied by tendencies toward anarchic models.

This book contributes to the debate on public administration, first, by providing a complete, updated, and in-depth analysis of the main bureaucratic and post-bureaucratic issues by reviewing and discussing previous literature on the theme.

Second, it contributes to the claim that effective change in the public sector should consider focusing on individuals and their behaviors, by employing a different approach to study and manage public organizations. Individuals represent the core of organizations, and the way they behave and interact may shape and define the way in which the organization itself behaves and carries out its activities. This issue is of key importance especially in public administration, where the involved interests affect a broad range of stakeholders.

Third, the findings emerging from the questionnaire support the understanding of the changes taking place in a country, such as Italy, that is part of the less regarded area, the Southern Europe, within studies on the public sector. In fact, findings emerging from the systematic review highlight the conclusion that past research has focused on Anglo-Saxon countries, while European countries, especially those in the Southern Europe area, are less regarded.

Fourth, because the questionnaire addresses crucial themes regarding the public sector, such as specialization, formalization, motivation, conflict, and managerial styles, it could be argued that this book has key implications for both academics and practitioners. Also, it might represent a first step of a more in-depth analysis of the perceptions held by individuals working in the public sector about their environment. This assessment, in turn, becomes crucial to individuate solutions to change those managerial practices and behaviors that are still rooted in the old approach to bureaucracy, which may be unhealthy both for public administrators and their stakeholders. In this way, the book provides concepts and empirical findings with implications useful for academics, public managers, and policy makers.

### References

Blau P.M., (1955), The dynamics of bureaucracy: a study of interpersonal relations in two Government Agencies, Chicago: University of Chicago Press.

Geddes L., (2012), In Search of Collaborative Public Management, *Public Management Review*, vol. 14, no. 7, pp. 947-966, doi: 10.1080/14719037.2011.650057.

Hinna A., Mameli S., Mangia G., (2016), *La pubblica amministrazione in movimento. Competenze, comportamenti e regole*, Milano: Egea.

Huse M. (2007). *Boards, Governance and Value Creation*, Cambridge: Cambridge University Press.

Klijn E.H. (2008), Complexity theory and Public Administration: what's new? Key concepts in complexity theory compared to their counterparts in public administration, *Public Management Review*, vol. 10, n. 3, pp. 299-317. doi: 10.1080/14719030802002675.

Kooiman J., Jentoft S. (2009), Meta-governance: values, norms and principles, and the making of hard choices, *Public Administration*, vol. 87, no. 4, pp. 818-836. doi: 10.1111/j.1467-9299.2009.01780.x.

Meek J.W., (2010), Complexity Theory for Public Administration and Policy, *Emergence: Complexity & Organization*, vol. 12, n. 1, pp. 1-4.

Merton R.K., (1940), Bureaucratic Structure and Personality, *Social Forces*, vol. 18, n. 4, pp. 560-568. doi: 10.2307/2570634.

Osborne S.P. (2010a), "The (New) Public Governance: a suitable case for treatment", Chap. 1 in *The New Public Governance?* London: Routledge.

Osborne S.P. (2010b), "Public governance and public service delivery: a research agenda for the future", Chap. 23 in *The New Public Governance?* London: Routledge.

Simon H. (1956), Rational choice and the structure of the environment, *Psychological Review*, vol. 63, n. 2, pp. 129-138.

Chapter 1

# POST-BUREAUCRATIC MODELS: A SYSTEMATIC LITERATURE REVIEW

## 1. Premise

This chapter proposes a systematic literature review to answer two fundamental, albeit inconclusively debated, questions.

Firstly, it aims to detect the limitations and concerns affecting public sector bureaucracies. Secondly, it seeks to describe the models possibly overcoming extant limitations and improving public sector organizations and administrations.

In finding answers to these questions, a fundamental premise is related to the issues of bureaucracy and complexity within the public sector, paying particular attention to those factors, both external and internal, which contribute to qualify public sector organizations as complex bureaucracies.

The second section discusses the features of complexity, also with reference to theories of complexity in public administration. The third section is then focused on discussing the characteristics of bureaucracy, its application within the public sector, and its main limitations. On these grounds – bearing in mind that the public sector is permeated by logics of power, politics, and complexity, and considering the importance of culture and context – the fourth section will discuss the first responses to bureaucracy that emerged in literature. The chapter will then explore more in detail how in recent years international literature has discussed new possible organizational models to solve the problems related to bureaucracy. In particular, it would be worth understanding how many studies have addressed the questions raised, especially taking into account the logics of power and politics, the importance of culture and context, and the role of complexity.

## 2. The phenomenon of complexity

Complexity is a central issue to be considered when addressing the problem of organizing public systems in an appropriate manner. In particular, complexity and the constraints that result from it must be interpreted appropriately in terms of actors and contingencies that might influence a certain process, thus avoiding the otherwise undeniable production of adverse effects on outcomes.

At first glance, complexity could be defined as the characteristic of a system conceived as an organic and structured aggregate of mutually interacting parts, according to which the overall behavior of the system is not immediately attributable to that of individual constituents, depending on the way in which they interact. Complex systems are thus systems "*comprised of numerous interacting identities (parts), each of which is behaving in its local context according to some rule(s), law(s) or force(s)*" (Maguire and McKelvey, 1999: 26). When the individual parts of complex systems (the agents) respond to their own local conditions, they cause the system as a whole to display emergent patterns, even if there is no deliberate coordination or communication between the parts (Maguire and McKelvey, 1999). In other words – and as many theories of complexity stress – systems are self-organizing and display emergent properties which cannot be traced to the behavior of the individual agents alone. These emergent properties and the relatively autonomous character of the agents cause systems to have unpredictable and complex dynamics. Thus, on one side, complexity should be declined in coherence with the specific context in which it has to be applied. On the other side, the concept of complexity facilitates discussion of the fact that it comprehends and explains well the need of a systemic vision that characterizes every economic system, including the public one.

More specifically, complex systems like public sector organizations are largely defined by interaction and communication. This includes interactions between the people within the organization, and the interactive communications flowing in and out of the system through its relationship with other organizations and through those people who enter and then leave the system (Haynes, 2015).

Therefore, since public systems are characterized by dynamic interactions among different actors, it is prominent advancing a discussion on the factors that characterize the concept of social complexity (Luhmann, 1995; McFarland, 1969). Social complexity may derive from varying degrees of interdependencies that exist among the different actors involved within a social system.

According to Luhmann (1995), the best sense we have of social structures derives from understanding the communications, or lack of communications, between systems and subsystems. Essentially, it is the closure of interaction, the failure of communication, explicitly or implicitly, intended or unintended, that is the defining feature of social and organizational life. Therefore, the marketplace (economics) and the justice system (law) can only be structurally coupled by certain formal methods and points of communication. Subsystems like the justice system work to reduce social complexity to make their own sphere of social operation manageable. One of the consequences is a closure with other subsystems.

Public managers operate in subsystems that are directed by rules, regulations, and procedures, but the interpretation of these is a vital component and different staff will interpret and prioritize them differently depending on their own role, or professional allegiance, in the organization. Managers experience the paradox of openness and closure that Luhmann defines, whereby horizontal and innovative work requires particular skills of communication if progress is to be made.

Complex systems are full of dynamic interactions from which the future state of the system emerges. Managers can take part in these interactions and thereby seek to influence the future of the system, but there are limits in their ability to determine outcomes and to control the direction that the emergence of new forms of order takes. The importance of recognizing changing interactions rather than assuming causations can be applied to an understanding of many historical debates about political problem definition and the role of policy development and public service interventions.

Complexity theory and its study of system dynamics puts much emphasis on feedback interactions (Meadows, 2009). Feedback is reinforcing (positive) or balancing (negative). Social scientists increasingly avoid the "positive" and "negative" labels, because they can be confused with normative value judgments, when the descriptions are intended as simple scientific language for observing system dynamics. Reinforcing and balancing feedbacks are important concepts for managers seeking to intervene in complex systems. They are responses to dynamic and unpredictable patterns and associations of human interactions. Poor judgments about when to respond to complex system dynamics can cause instability and social problems. In fact, the level of stability/variability of a system is an additional possible source of positive or negative influence on the degree of complexity of the system itself.

Finally, complexity may also result from the subjective perceptions of individuals embedded within the system. Thus, factors of social complexity can be related to certain structural or functional characteristics, both to the cognitive limits that the system actors perceive and to a combination of these elements.

By putting an accent on the sociological view of complexity, it is useful to highlight that public organizations are complex by their nature, since they are embedded in a complex system and they produce complexity, exist in complexity, and feed on complexity (Baccarani, 2010). The public organization, as a social and vital system, relies on internal and external relationships and on the search for survival in long-term horizons through the interactions between the structural and functional elements that make them up, the individuals and the social and environmental systems in which they are embedded.

It is widely acknowledged that the turbulence and uncertainty that characterize modern contexts, along with the increased competitiveness and the unpredictability of markets, are progressively leading to a need for new models within the public sector tending toward ever more open and dynamic systems, characterized by de-structured and less hierarchical organizational forms, based on high diversity and variability, with open, reticulated, and flexible boundaries.

Thus, the new model of public organization should take into account that its success and survival are now necessarily based on the acknowledgment and acclamation of the elements of diversity among individuals, on a constant, cooperative, and co-competitive exchange, on communication, on the development of long-term relationships with stakeholders, and on a great permeability and responsiveness to change and innovation (Kale and Singh, 2007; Nonaka, 1994; Powell et al., 2005).

## 3. The phenomenon of bureaucracy

In its pure form, bureaucracy has been described by Weber (1922) as the most efficient and rational way of organizing. According to the author, bureaucratization is the key part of the rational-legal authority; furthermore, he saw it as the key process in the ongoing rationalization of the Western society. He argued, in fact, that bureaucratic coordination of activities was the distinctive mark of the modern era.

In his study, Weber individuated several preconditions for the emergence of bureaucracy: the growth in space and population being administered; the growth in complexity of the administrative tasks being carried out; and the existence of a monetary economy requiring a more efficient administrative system. Offices are thus ranked in a hierarchical order and their operations are characterized by impersonal rules, while appointments are made according to specialized qualifications.

There was the belief that a system of transparent rules was better than a system without rules. Weber's typical ideal bureaucracy is characterized by hierarchical organization; delineated lines of authority in a fixed area of activity; action taken on the basis of, and recorded in, written rules; bureaucratic officials needing expert training; rules implemented by neutral officials; career advancement made through public competitions; and is based on technical qualifications.

Weber clarifies that both the public and private bureaucracy are based on specific competencies of various offices. These competencies are specified in various rules, laws, and administrative regulations. This means that:

- There is a rigid division of labor.
- A chain of command is established in which the capacity to coerce is specified and restricted by regulations.
- There is a regular and continuous execution of the assigned tasks by people qualified by education and training to perform them.

This bureaucratic coordination of the actions of large numbers of people became the dominant structural feature of then modern forms of organization. This organizational model allows large-scale planning, and becomes particularly fitting for mass production, where there is a need to perform numerous repeated and standardized activities. The same is true for those particularly rigid contexts, where workers are not asked for particular competences and training, thus allowing managers and executives easily to centralize control and exert their power.

According to Weber, the bureaucratic organization is the privileged mean that has shaped the modern polity, the modern economy, and the modern technology. Bureaucratic types of organization are seen by Weber as technically superior to all other forms of administration, much as machine production is superior to handicraft methods. Moreover, as time passed and the external context changed, several problems and limitations of this model emerged.

Nowadays the term "bureaucracy" has become synonymous with "inefficiency", following failure in several of its premises. During the 1940s and 1950s, literature already started to advance some negative aspects emerging from the application of bureaucratic models.

Weber himself provided some dysfunctions of bureaucracy. While recognizing bureaucracy as the most efficient form of organization – and even indispensable for the modern state – Weber saw it as a threat to individual freedoms, and the ongoing bureaucratization as leading to a *"polar night of icy darkness"* (Weber, 1946, 128) in which increasing rationalization of human life traps individuals in a soulless "iron cage" of bureaucratic, rule-based, rational control. Its major advantage, the calculability of results, also renders it a model unable to deal with individual cases, leading to phenomena of depersonalization. Thus, modern rationalized and bureaucratized systems of law have become incapable of dealing with individual particularities to which earlier types of justice were well suited.

Merton (1940) introduced the concept of "displacement of goals", whereby *"an instrumental value becomes a terminal value"* (p. 563). According to the author, by following bureaucracy's principles and rules, bureaucrats arrived at a situation in which the rules became the goals instead of the process or service to be delivered. While Merton agreed with certain aspects of Weber's analysis, he also considered the dysfunctional aspects of bureaucracy, which he attributed to a "trained incapacity" resulting from "overconformity". He saw bureaucrats as more likely to defend their own entrenched interests than to act to benefit the organization as a whole. He further believed that bureaucrats took pride in their craft, which led them to resist changes in established routines. Merton also noted that bureaucrats emphasized formality over interpersonal relationships, and had been trained to ignore the special circumstances of particular cases, causing them to come across as "arrogant" and "haughty".

Similarly, Selznick (1948) suggests that bureaucrats' excessive focus on personal goals rather than on those of the organization leads to a bifurcation of interests that hinders the efficient way of doing things.

Blau (1955) emerged as another interesting critic of bureaucracy in relation to the concept of "work to rule", a trade union tactic according to which employees adopt behaviors to do nothing more than the minimum required by the rules of their contract: they precisely follow all regulations, which may cause a slowdown or decrease in productivity. This behavior can be better translated into "hiding behind the rules", meaning that the rule becomes a way of justifying something that has not been done by employees.

In brief, critiques of the bureaucratic model can be considered under four aspects, covering both internal and external aspects:

• Economic: inefficiency and low performances.
• Organizational: low motivation of employees; turnover; alienation; lack of human resources policies; lack of flexibility.
• Social: episodes of corruption; absenteeism; opportunism.
• Institutional: low attention paid to citizens; citizens are much more passive (users) than active (customers); poor quality of public services delivered.

These critiques become more relevant if contextualized in a much more modern world, demanding more flexibility. The higher complexity characterizing the modern world requires organizational models and lean procedures able to adapt to a new and ever-changing context.

Even in literature (e.g., Klijn, 2008; Meek, 2010), this limit has been repeatedly acknowledged, especially emphasizing that public systems are still strongly anchored to an ancient tradition of bureaucratic, standardized, and repeated activities characterized by high rationality (Meek, 2010).

Indeed, as well known from Simon's studies (1956), it is impossible to consider the existence of a perfect rationality, which means that rational behaviors, even in the public sector, should be considered more as an exception rather than be taken for granted (Klijn, 2008). This is more even true in a particularly complex context such as the public.

## 4. First responses to bureaucracy in literature

In literature, considering elements related to control and flexibility or adaptability, two main approaches to the problem of performance management in public bureaucracies are evidenced (Kettl, 1997). The following table shows the key points of the two approaches.

**Table 1.1.** The two main approaches to solve performance issues within bureaucracies.

| Approaches | Optimizing Bureaucracy | Reflexive Bureaucracy |
|---|---|---|
| **Emphasis** | Static efficiency, focus on minimizing costs and increasing productivity. | Continuous learning and reviewing; focus on quality, impact and sustainability of actions to solve problems. |
| **Characteristics of the goals and objectives** | Predetermined; singular; focus on specific goals prioritizing), generating reductionism and myopia. | Temporary and under constant review; attention to interrelationships between multiple objectives (the complex natureof the problems). |
| **Relationship between performance evaluation and execution of tasks** | External evaluation, formal objective. | Embedded evaluation, contextual substantive. |
| **Relationship between "front line" and administrative centers** | Individual (solitary) and evaluative, based on specific criteria and indicators; two possible outcomes: compliance or deviation. | Deliberative (group), involving justification processes (explaining behaviors and results produced from the actual experience of implementation). |
| **Relationship with uncertainties/dealing with "the unexpected"** | Tendency to treat the new and unexpected as if they were variations of pre-established routines (categorical framework) or exceptions. | Unexpected occurrences are constantly problematized for detecting problems and correcting errors; diffusion of innovations. |

*Source:* own re-elaboration from Pires, 2010.

The first approach is guided by the "principle of optimization" and is based on the assumption of the separation between the moments and instances of decision-making, implementation, and evaluation of actions taken by bureaucrats (i.e., separation of means and ends). In this approach, activities and people are evaluated by adopting objective criteria that are far from being related to the substantive contexts of task execution (e.g., decisions, behaviors, and practices in each situation or specific case). For instance, the task of performance management will require the establishment of mechanisms and evaluation systems that are independent and external from the specific task execution. These systems generally consist of formal procedures, such as indicators and quantitative targets, which serve as external – and supposedly objective – parameters to judge the success or failure of the actions executed. The main objective of these systems is to promote greater efficiency by minimizing costs and increasing productivity in the implementation of a restricted set of objectives and results. On the other hand, linking evaluation to objective parameters enables a process of discharge of responsibility, since public managers may hide their decisions behind formal rules and procedures determined *a priori*.

Under this first approach falls the New Public Management (NPM) (Hood, 1991). The NPM emerged after a decade of public spending reductions as an idea of managerializing public services, using new structures, and adopting mixed (network and market) governances. In the context of state failure, of poor performance of its bureaucracies, and of the widespread discontent with the actions of governments, the NPM approach brought to the center of the debate the concern over performance in the public sector. With its focus on results and on optimizing the public budget, the managerial approach promised improvements in bureaucratic efficiency and accountability following agency theory, through the creation of incentive systems that would direct bureaucrats (the agents) to meet the targets set by policy makers, political representatives, and citizens (principals) in the provision of public goods and services. Trying to overcome the mistakes of the past, such as the emphasis on procedural controls, the managerialist proposal introduces into the public context the concepts that have always driven the private sector: the imposition of goals and indicators to measure the performance of organizations and their workers, a strong emphasis on incentives based on payments, and performance-related pay systems. Under this model, public sector organizations should focus on a set of performance goals that can be defined in a specific form, being quantifiable and measurable. Each bureaucrat in the organization should achieve part of the overall goal. Supervisors constantly monitor the performance of their bureaucrats in terms of achieving those goals, taking as references indicators of quantitative results. In order to correctly manage incentives, managers distribute bonuses to those employees who periodically meet the established goals.

Despite the appealing premises and promises, assessments of the implementation of managerial reforms around the world have led to paradoxical results. On the one hand, there is evidence of increased productivity; on the other hand, increases in productivity in relation to some specific indicators have also been accompanied by the perception of problems related to the maintenance of satisfactory levels of motivation and commitment by government employees. For example, some studies (Chalkley et al., 2010; Houston, 2000) have demonstrated that performance-based systems involving pecuniary incentives may contribute to increasing productivity, but, in general, they lead to significant losses of intrinsic motivation from professionals – that is, the motivation derived from values, commitment, and a sense of mission in relation to work, as opposed to extrinsic motivation based on rewards not substantially related to work, like money.

In addition, another line of problems identified with managerialist reforms refers to the distortions provoked by the incentive systems implemented. A considerable volume of scholarly work has pointed out the dysfunctional effects of quantitative and predefined performance measurements (Bouckaert and Balk, 1991; Dunleavy and Hood, 1994). Firstly, the specification of quantifiable performance goals necessarily results in an excessive reductionism of what is expected to be the state's (and its bureaucracies') role. Goal-setting tends to limit and focus the actions taken by organizations around very specific and narrow points, reducing employees' abilities to understand and address problems in a broader fashion.

Besides the question of reductionism provoked by the predetermination and pre-specification of results, the measurement and quantitative standardization of these results frequently lead bureaucrats to find ways to convert the activities that they are used to doing into the very products and goals pursued by their supervisors. An indicative example of this is the "creative accounting" that takes place in the recording of activities performed by employees. Supposedly undesirable results can be easily codified in terms of desired outcomes – for example, in order to reduce waiting lists, employees can create a waiting list for the waiting list. These situations show that management systems of this type are not immune to manipulation of the measurement process and to the manipulation of organizational products, in both cases promoting dysfunctional behaviors from the viewpoint of the effectiveness of the actions taken by public bureaucracies.

In other words, a wide and diverse body of evidence has pointed out the side-effects of performance evaluation systems based on the managerialist approach.

Based on these negative evidences, even analysts and academics who sympathize with the model have recognized that reforms inspired by the managerialist approach have failed to deliver the expectations of a more effective and efficient public administration (Dunleavy et al., 2006; Hood and Peters, 2004).

A second approach considers the "principle of reflexivity". According to the concept of reflexive bureaucracy (Mintzberg, 1979), a public administration should successfully complete the processes entrusted to it, while developing skills and behaviors that can make it reflect on the organization's functioning. This approach differs from the previous one by rejecting the distinction between decisions, implementation, and evaluation, and emphasizing the need for performance to be assessed in a contextualized manner, as an activity embedded in the actual context of implementation of activities (substantive judgment).

Moreover, the reflective approach also rejects the simplifying assumptions of human behavior in which incentive systems for performance are based on the perception that individuals (or groups and organizations) are motivated by the desire to obtain rewards (such as money or status) and avoid sanctions. Thus, in this second approach, the task of managing performance involves the establishment of routines that enable agents to reflect and review ongoing activities and bureaucratic actions, so that monitoring performance is itself part of a wider process of institutional innovation and learning.

Significant research after the middle of the 2000s argued that a post-NPM epoch might be dawning. Lapsley (2008, 2009) set out a series of unresolved contradictions in the NPM approach, arguing that the NPM failed to deliver better value, since proponents underestimate the complexity permeating the public sector. An alternative perspective that has emerged is that new forms of governance were superseding managerialism (Kooiman and Jentoft, 2009). Osborne (2010a, 2010b), in fact, put new public governances (NPG) at the center of a post-NPM debate, based on involving more actors (both public and private), creating more consensus and voluntary participation in decision-making processes, and establishing collaborative relationships and networks.

However, it should be acknowledged that the results of this approach were weaker than those of the previous one, since trends such as 'new public management' (Hood, 1991), 'performance oriented management' (Pollitt and Bouckaert, 2000) and the rise of the 'audit society' (Power, 1999) indicate that the world of public management has now become, first and foremost, a world of measurement (Noordegraaf and Abma, 2003).

The concept of measurement opens up two main issues. On one side, under a prospective point of view, measurement enables the establishment of tight, objectified links between objectives, means, outputs, and out-comes, and thus the establishment of transparent administration. On the other side, retrospectively, it enables the evaluation of organizational out-puts and outcomes, and thus the strengthening of effective administration. In both ways, public management comes to be considered as a matter of 'management by measurement' (Noordegraaf and Abma, 2003). However, the results of this approach are reductive in respect of the wider and more complex world that the public sector is. Issues regarding the public may not be limited only to matters of measurement, rules, or procedures, but rather should address problems of transparency, accountability, and man-agement practices.

In any case, what clearly results from this first general review of the lit-erature is that there is great confusion about what kind of intervention is really needed in the public sector to find a solution to the emerging prob-lems. With the aim of giving an order to these concepts and shedding light on the main issues to be overcome, the following sections 5 and 6 address a systematic literature review, while section 7 discusses the results, highlights the emerging gaps, and proposes possible solutions.

## 5. Research method

In order to assess the state-of-the-art of international literature on bu-reaucracy and post-bureaucracy approaches and to search for answers to the research questions (see section 1), a systematic literature review has been conducted through ISI Web of Knowledge (Thomson Reuters re-search engine). Results have been then integrated by also searching key-words on the websites of journals resulting from the first search. In total, 23 journals, as listed in Box 1.1, have been reviewed.

**Box 1.1.** Journals reviewed.

| |
|---|
| *American Behavioral Scientist* |
| *Australian Health Review* |
| *BMC Health Services Research* |
| *British Journal of Management* |
| *European Journal of Public Health* |
| *European Management Journal* |
| *Health Policy* |
| *Health Services Management Research* |
| *International Journal of Public Sector Management* |

*see next page*

*International Public Management Journal*
*Journal of Community Psychology*
*Journal of Health Organization and Management*
*Journal of Knowledge Management*
*Journal of Management Studies*
*Journal of Public Administration Research and Theory*
*Local Government Studies*
*Management Decision*
*Organization Studies*
*Policing – An International Journal of Police Strategies & Management*
*Public Administration*
*Public Administration Review*
*Public Management Review*
*Public Management: An International Journal of Research and Theory*

The review process has been structured following five steps identified by Khan et al. (2003) to conduct an effective systematic literature review. The five steps consist of:

1. Framing questions for a review, by establishing useful keywords.
2. Eliminating duplicates and identifying relevant studies by selecting titles and abstracts.
3. Assessing the quality of studies by analyzing full papers.
4. Summarizing the evidence.
5. Interpreting the findings.

The following keywords have been selected to search for studies focusing on the main post-bureaucratic models in the public sector: "post-bureaucracy", "professional bureaucracy", "reflexive bureaucracy", "New Public Management", and "New Public Governance". Publication years have been selected starting from 1991.

In step 1, by typing these keywords, 665 articles emerged from ISI Web of Knowledge and from single journal research engines. Proceedings papers (365), article reviews (49), book reviews (55), and meeting abstracts (30) have not been considered within the aim of this study. Thus, from the first step, 166 articles were selected.

After eliminating duplicates, the second step consisted of selecting relevant studies by searching the focus of the papers according to titles and then abstracts, using other specific keywords related to the aim of the review. The keywords used were "public", "professional", "bureaucracy", "reflexive", "administration", "government", and "management". This step yielded 95 articles.

The full-text analysis in step 3 looked for article coherence by searching for the effective focus on new models of bureaucracy within public sector. The final database is composed of 68 relevant articles.

Finally, step 4 and step 5 consisted of summarizing, interpreting, and re-elaborating findings, as discussed in the following section. Specifically, several critical areas of discussion were identified: type of public organization/administration observed, country observed, characteristics and critiques applied to other approaches/models, and authors' proposal to improve PA models.

Once the main characteristics of each study were identified, a Pearson's correlation test was used to verify existing relationships among approach, year, country, and public administration observed.

Approach, country, and PA have been treated as polychotomous variables (approach_NPM, approach_NPG, approach_hybrid, approach_behavioral; country_AngloSaxon, country_NorthCenterEurope, country_SouthEurope; PA_Health SocialCare, PA_Education, PA_Local_government, PA_Central_government), while the year has been treated as a continuous variable.

## 6. Results

Results from the analysis show a surprising concentration of contributions between 2005 and 2011 (37), while previously and subsequently only few papers proved to be relevant to the aim of this work, that being to analyze papers focusing on post-bureaucratic models to detect critiques of and solutions to previous models. In fact, during the period characterized by the rise of NPM (1991-2006) 28 papers were found to be relevant for this review, while in the period after 2006 (New Public Governance), 40 papers proved to be relevant.

**Figure 1.1.** Literature review results per year of publication.

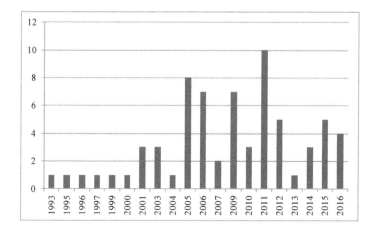

Not including 11 studies that analyzed public administration models only from a theoretical point of view, works presenting empirical cases showed a strong tendency to consider Anglo-Saxon countries, as can be seen from the following table.

**Table 1.2.** Empirical studies per country.

| Macro-Area | Country | N |
|---|---|---|
| Anglo-Saxon countries | UK (England, Wales, Scotland) | 25 |
| | Ireland | 1 |
| | USA | 4 |
| | Canada | 1 |
| | Australia | 5 |
| | New Zealand | 1 |
| North and Central European countries | Norway | 1 |
| | Denmark | 2 |
| | Sweden | 1 |
| | The Netherlands | 5 |
| | Belgium | 2 |
| | Germany | 4 |
| | Austria | 2 |
| | France | 3 |
| South European countries | Italy | 4 |
| | Portugal | 3 |
| | Spain | 2 |
| | Greece | 1 |
| Other countries | South Korea | 2 |
| | Ethiopia | 1 |

Anglo-Saxon countries have been used as empirical cases in 37 papers, while North and Continental European countries have been analyzed 20 times. South European countries have been studied only in ten papers. Table 1.2 clearly shows a significant focus on Anglo-Saxon countries and a lack of attention toward European countries, in particular toward those from the Southern part.

Focusing on the type of public administration observed, Table 1.3 gives insights into the specific cases analyzed. Nineteen papers are generally focused on the public sector.

**Table 1.3.** Focus per public administration observed.

| PA observed | N |
|---|---|
| Local government | 16 |
| Central government | 3 |
| Health and social care | 24 |
| Education (schools and universities) | 5 |
| Public agencies | 1 |

Table 1.3 clearly shows the significant focus on the study of health and social care institutions and local government, with less attention paid to central government and education institutes.

An interesting analysis could then be to consider the approach informing the studies resulting from the systematic review. To this aim, the main approaches can refer to classic bureaucracy, reflexive bureaucracy, professional bureaucracy, New Public Management ("optimizing bureaucracy"), collaborative or representative governance (going toward the NPG approach), and hybridization.

Studies under the label "classic bureaucracy" are those that still refer to a model of public administration based on rules, standardization, and a strong hierarchy, or even those studies that suggest only small improvements to the classic bureaucracy but not considering a radical change of the organizational model.

Studies under the label "reflexive bureaucracy" are those focusing on models that consider learning from the past, listening, experiencing, and thinking.

Studies under the label "professional bureaucracy" are those referring to the need to improve professionals' managerial competences, increase professionals' autonomy and include professionals within the top management team.

Studies under the label "New Public Management" are those giving attention to themes such as evaluation, efficiency, and performance following lessons from private sector management.

Studies under the label "New Public Governance" are those papers focusing on themes such as collaboration, participation, and stakeholders' involvement.

Finally, studies under the label "hybridization" are those concentrating on the development of hybrid forms of public administration, adopting arrangements between markets, collaboration, and steering, or solutions combining traditional bureaucracy with increased flexibility and user focus.

Table 1.4 reports the categorization of papers per approach. Four papers were found not to adopt a specific approach, since they did not advance any significant proposal to solve the limitations emerging from other models.

**Table 1.4.** Categorization of papers per approach.

| Approach | N |
|---|---|
| Classic bureaucracy | 5 |
| Professional bureaucracy | 5 |
| Reflexive bureaucracy | 7 |
| NPM | 15 |
| NPG, collaborative and representative | 19 |
| Hybridization | 10 |
| Behavioral | 3 |

*Source:* classification adapted from Osborne (2006).

The table shows a great focus on approaches related to New Public Management and New Public Governance, thus witnessing that at least within the academic debate there has been a move toward the analysis of post-bureaucratic models founded on radical changes, differently from the professional and the reflexive approaches that rather focus on small changes in respect of the classic approach to bureaucracy.

In addition to the six categories identified, one more category has been inserted in the table: the behavioral approach. Only three papers were found to fall within this category, focusing on the micro-dimension related to the analysis of bureaucrats' work and their behaviors, and giving rise to the need to adopt this approach to better catch the nuances of bureaucratic work and its effects on the performance of the public administration, not only in terms of economic performance and efficiency, but even in terms of accountability and of results to be gained in the public interest.

Given the high number of studies using the NPM approach and the high focus on Anglo-Saxon countries, a Pearson's correlation test was used to verify the existence of a relationship among the approach, the year, the country, and the public administration observed.

Table 1.5 shows results from the correlation test, where Country AS are Anglo-Saxon countries, Country NCE are North and Central European countries, and Country SE are South European countries.

**Table 1.5.** Pearson's correlation test between approach, year, country, and PA observed.

| | Correlations | | | | | | | | | | |
|---|---|---|---|---|---|---|---|---|---|---|---|
| | 1 | 2 | 3 | 4 | 5 | 6 | 7 | 8 | 9 | 10 | 11 |
| 1. Approach NPM | 1 | | | | | | | | | | |
| 2. Approach NPG | -0.327** | 1 | | | | | | | | | |
| 3. Approach hybrid | -0.207 | -0.222 | 1 | | | | | | | | |
| 4. Approach behavioral | -0.114 | -0.123 | -0.078 | 1 | | | | | | | |
| 5. Year | -0.241* | 0.194 | 0.294* | -0.03 | 1 | | | | | | |
| 6. Country AS | -0.04 | 0.086 | -0.047 | 0.066 | -0.054 | 1 | | | | | |
| 7. Country NCE | 0.098 | -0.014 | 0.05 | 0.028 | -0.003 | -0.623** | 1 | | | | |
| 8. Country SE | -0.141 | -0.075 | 0.075 | -0.087 | 0.137 | -0.427** | -0.259* | 1 | | | |
| 9. PA Health Social Care | -0.116 | -0.099 | 0.206 | 0.114 | 0.167 | 0.073 | -0.122 | -0.029 | 1 | | |
| 10. PA Education | 0.236* | -0.037 | -0.102 | -0.056 | -0.136 | 0.051 | 0.077 | -0.114 | -0.22 | 1 | |
| 11. PA Local Gov. | -0.057 | 0.139 | 0.003 | 0.057 | -0.044 | -0.007 | 0.046 | -0.131 | -0.430** | -0.144 | 1 |
| 12. PA Central Gov. | -0.092 | 0.092 | -0.063 | -0.035 | 0.043 | 0.166 | -0.103 | -0.071 | -0.136 | -0.046 | -0.089 |

*\*\* Correlation is significant at the 0.01 level (2-tailed).*
*\* Correlation is significant at the 0.05 level (2-tailed).*

Results interestingly show that there is a negative correlation between year and NPM approach (– 0.327 with $p < 0.01$) and a positive correlation between year and hybrid approach (0.294 with $p < 0.05$). This result may demonstrate that there is a recent trend going toward the hybrid approach, while the NPM approach has received less attention in more recent years.

Another interesting result shows that the NPM approach is positively correlated with public administrations in education (0.236 with $p < 0.05$).

Finally, it is also worth noting that, despite the literature usually tending to underline an existing correlation between the approach used and the country observed, no significant correlation has been found in this sense within this study; also, no correlation has been found between the approach and the specific public administration observed.

The following sub-sections provide for each model a specific explanation of solutions identified by the authors. Each sub-section will analyze the approach, the critiques offered, and the solutions proposed by the authors.

## 6.1. The classic bureaucracy

Studies focusing on the classic approach basically refer to the fact that post-bureaucracies failed in reaching several of the promised aims, and that solutions to solve main issues regarding the public sector can be found by simply reforming the classic bureaucratic model with small changes. They are basically contextualized between 2006 and 2009, apparently at the end of the lifecycle of the NPM approach and at the starting point of the NPG.

**Table 1.6.** Studies focusing on classic bureaucracy.

| Authors | PA observed | Country | Critiques of other models/approaches | Main proposals |
|---|---|---|---|---|
| Alexander et al. (2011) | Local government | Australia | - | Development of networks to improve the relationships among bureaucrats. |
| Kane and Patapan (2006) | N/A | Australia | NPM introduced contradictory aims that failed to take into account the problem of prudence. | Modern bureaucracies should be reformed in light of prudence. |
| Mengistu and Vogel (2006) | Health and social care | Ethiopia | Bureaucracy is an obstacle to the development of democracy due to behaviors oriented to rent-seeking and lack of representativeness. | Bureaucracy should be accompanied by good governance based on transparency and a clear hierarchy of objectives. Building a "neutral bureaucracy" to reduce rent-seeking and improve representativeness. |
| Pollitt (2009) | Health and social care | UK | Post-bureaucratic forms of organization perform less well than traditional bureaucracies with respect both to organizational memory and learning from experience; they tend to produce compressed decision-making processes which are more careless of history and experience than was the norm under traditional bureaucracy. For all their hypothesized benefits in terms of flexibility, post-bureaucratic public sector organizations may well make more avoidable mistakes, unintentionally damage existing strengths, pursue false and glib historical analogies, and muddy the trail of public accountability. | - |

*see next page*

| Zafirovski (2001) | N/A | N/A | Public choice theory – namely, the 'assumption that all individuals maximize only their own expected utility' – is unrealistic and leads to certain problems for the theory applying it.' | Reconsidering the description of bureaucrats and public administrators as complex agents rather than simple minded maximizers. |
|---|---|---|---|---|

Pollitt (2009) argues that post-bureaucratic forms of organization were seen to perform less well than traditional bureaucracies with respect both to organizational memory and learning from experience. As a result of this, they tend to produce compressed decision-making processes which are more careless of history and experience than was the norm under traditional bureaucracy. In searching for all the hypothesized benefits in terms of flexibility, post-bureaucratic organizations may well make more avoidable mistakes, unintentionally damage existing strengths, pursue false and glib historical analogies, and muddy the trail of public accountability (Pollitt, 2009).

Kane and Patapan (2006) contend that classic bureaucracy only needs to be reformed by following the principle of prudence, since the bureaucratic model has to be considered better than the one following the NPM principles. According to the authors, NPM in fact introduced contradictory aims that failed to take into account the problem of prudence, such as: to increase political control over bureaucracy and to free managers to manage (while simultaneously empowering service consumers); to promote flexibility and innovation and to increase citizen trust and governmental legitimacy; to give priority to savings and to improve performance; to make government more responsible and to reduce the range of tasks that government undertakes.

Mengistu and Vogel (2006) put the accent on the need to adopt good governance based on transparency within classic bureaucracies, to avoid the risk of rent-seeking, and to build a neutral bureaucracy that increases the degree of representativeness.

## 6.2. The professional bureaucracy

Professional bureaucracy is a model that finds its main application in those public organizations where the public interest meets certain professional activities, such as in the case of universities and healthcare organizations.

Studies falling under this approach mainly recognize as solutions to solve other models' failures the need for more professional autonomy within the public organization (e.g., Germov, 2005), and for increased involvement of professionals in the decision-making process or participation and inclusion in the top management team. The papers are chronologically spread over time, since there are contributions both during the 1990s and during the 2000s.

**Table 1.7.** Studies focusing on professional bureaucracy.

| Authors | PA observed | Country | Critiques of other models/approaches | Main proposals |
|---------|-------------|---------|--------------------------------------|----------------|
| Germov (2005) | Health and social care | Australia | The incorporation of NPM principles into professional practice placed constraints upon professional autonomy. | Increasing professionals' autonomy. |
| Kothari and Handscombe (2007) | Education | UK | Universities are based on the old bureaucratic approach that standardizes processes and knowledge. | Universities, as professional bureaucracies, should move toward transferable life skills such as numeracy, problem-solving, IT, communication, and working with others in teams. |
| Lega and DePietro (2005) | Health and social care | France, UK, Italy, Germany, and Spain | Organizational models in healthcare are converging toward bureaucratized professionals. | Develop adequate managerial competences, design a coherent organizational structure, and develop performance-based systems (PBS) not only related to financial performances. |
| Tichelar (1997) | Local government | - | Bureaucracy is characterized by alienation, dehumanization, coercion; professional bureaucracies characterized by the state contract and self-regulation models are scarcely receptive to innovatory change processes. | Professional bureaucracies should put the emphasis on openness and consensus rather than control and coercion. |
| Vinot (2014) | Health and social care | France | The NPM approach sees a manager coordinating the activities carried out by professionals, but this might engender conflicts among the two roles within "professional bureaucracies" such as hospitals. | Professional bureaucracies work at their best when professionals are involved in the change process. |

For instance, Vinot (2014) highlights that professional bureaucracies work at their best when professionals are involved in the change process. The author criticizes the NPM approach since it sees a manager coordinating the activities carried out by professionals, and this might engender conflicts among the two roles within professional bureaucracies such as hospitals, thus worsening organizational performance.

Kothari and Handscombe (2007), indeed, offer a critique against those universities adopting the classic model of bureaucracy in place of the professional model. The critique underlines that bureaucracy standardizes processes and knowledge, while universities should adopt a professional model that enhances the development of transferable life skills such as numeracy, problem-solving, IT, communication, and working with others in teams.

Tichelar (1997) criticizes that bureaucracy is characterized by alienation, dehumanization, and coercion, and that professional bureaucracies characterized by the state contract and self-regulation models are scarcely receptive to innovatory change processes. Indeed, according to the author, professional bureaucracies can find solutions by putting the emphasis on openness and consensus rather than control and coercion.

Lega and DePietro (2005) contend that a possible solution within professional bureaucracies is the development of adequate managerial competences, the design of a coherent organizational structure, and the provision of performance-based systems not only related to financial performance.

## 6.3. The reflexive bureaucracy

The reflexive approach comprises those studies focusing on models that consider concepts such as learning from the past, listening, experiencing, and thinking. Works falling within this category contend that organizations should reflect and learn from previous experiences to better perform in the future. Contributions within this category were mainly published between 2009 and 2012.

**Table 1.8.** Studies focusing on reflexive bureaucracy.

| Authors | PA observed | Country | Critiques of other models/approaches | Main proposals |
|---|---|---|---|---|
| Considine (2000) | - | UK, Netherlands, New Zealand and Australia | Bureaucracy can no longer cope with the pressures being put on it by budget restraints, higher client expectations, and claims of inflexibility by interest groups and political elites. Bureaucracy is related to collusion, fraud, and lack of accountability. | Contract regimes and reflexive interactions may hinder the public programs from being delivered. |
| Esmark (2009) | N/A | N/A | Previous discussions within governance research have interpreted the process of functional differentiation as a process of accelerated change and increased diversity, fragmentation, and complexity, which in turn is seen to drive a proliferation of network-based governance in public policy processes. | New forms of reflexive and network-based governance as a supplement to conventional instruments of governance such as order and command, legal instructions, and coercion. |
| Gourdin and Schepers (2009) | Health and social care | Belgium | Professional bureaucracies lead to a loss or anyway to a transformation of professional autonomy due to the service standardization. | Organizations need to integrate professional knowledge by following a principle of reflexivity. |
| Kinder (2012) | Local government | Scotland | NPM approach emphasizes exogenous knowledge transfer and decenters the importance of staff playing active conscious roles in innovation processes. | New approaches should consider learning in organizations much more likely to produce transformative service models and continuous innovation than passive learning; the response to old models should be grounded on practices, listening, and learning. |
| Magone (2011) | N/A | Portugal | Bureaucracy centralizes decision-making and provides inefficient human resource allocation; low level of qualifications. | Adopting a holistic and reflexive governance approach, based on administrative learning from the past, open-ended feedback structure on reforms, and engagement of public stakeholders. |

*see next page*

| Orr and Vince (2009) | Local government | UK | - | Adopting a reflexive approach which is contingently and differentially experienced, that should take into account that traditions feed and sustain assumptions about goals, values, behaviors, orientation toward the outside world, the allocation of different kinds of resources, the assessment of performance, and processes of leadership development. |
|---|---|---|---|---|
| Rothstein and Downer (2012) | Central government | UK | Bureaucracy leads to a lack of efficiency, control, and accountability. | Setting up a risk-based management of public administration to get closer to concepts of 'trust' and 'precaution'; new approaches should think about the emergence of risk as a dominant organizing concept for policymaking and its relationship with changing institutional patterns of transparency, accountability, and blame. |

For instance, Orr and Vince (2009) highlight that a solution to the failure of previous models should be found in a reflexive dynamic which is contingently and differentially experienced. This approach should consider that traditions feeding and sustaining assumptions about goals, values, behaviors, orientation toward the outside world, the allocation of different kinds of resources, the assessment of performance, and processes of leadership development.

Several authors (Gourdin and Schepers, 2009; Kinder, 2012), with the same advice, criticize the NPM approach since it emphasizes exogenous knowledge transfer and decentralizes the importance of staff playing active conscious roles in innovation processes. According to Kinder (2012), for example, the response to old models should be grounded on practice, listening, and learning: new approaches should consider learning in organizations that is much more likely to produce transformative service models and continuous innovation rather than considering passive learning.

According to Considine (2000), the failure of the classic bureaucracy in relation to collusion, fraud, and lack of accountability should be overcome by contract regimes and reflexive interactions to ensure the public programs to be delivered. In addition to this, Rothstein and Downer (2012) argue that the lack of accountability and control finds a solution by setting up a risk-based management to get closer to such concepts as trust and precaution, thinking about the emergence of the risk as the dominant concept for policymaking and its relationship with public stakeholders.

## 6.4. The New Public Management

The New Public Management approach mainly finds its roots in the application of private sector management principles about the need for evaluation, the search for efficiency and performance. Contributions in this category cover the whole of the observed period (1991-2016), thus confirming Noordegraaf and Abma's (2003) assertion that the public sector has become, first and foremost, a world of measurement.

**Table 1.9.** Studies focusing on New Public Management.

| Authors | PA observed | Country | Critiques of other models/approaches | Main proposals |
|---|---|---|---|---|
| Ahn and Bretschneider (2011) | Local government | South Korea | Bureaucracy is based on rules and regulations that tend to be unresponsive to the demands of citizens. It also implies a low level of consultation and communication with citizens and a high level of communication distortion. | e-Government applications enhance improvements in terms of accountability, responsiveness and transparency. |
| Charlesworth et al. (1996) | Health and social care | UK | Professionalism for its definitional and institutional imperialism; bureaucracy for its inflexibility and impersonality; political representation for its intrusive ideology and dogma. | Managerial approach based on market principles, customer-centeredness, flexibility, and good business practices. |
| De Boer et al. (2007) | Education | The Netherlands | - | Communicative-planning and network approaches. |
| Hammerschmid and Meyer (2005) | Local government | Austria | NPM reforms produced a significant archetype change in the Austrian public sector. | - |

*see next page*

| Kickert (2005) | - | France, Germany, Italy | NPM lacks account-ability and shows an excessive managerial autonomy. | Improve democratic and political accountability and control. |
|---|---|---|---|---|
| Kickert (2011) | - | Greece, Italy, Portugal, Spain | Bureaucracy is charac-terized by immobilism and inertia, formalism, clientelism, patronage and corruption; NPM reforms led to very small changes; no sub-stantial changes oc-curred. | - |
| Kirkpatrick (1999) | Education | UK | The application of NPM principles leads to conflicting results: in some cas-es, it produces no effects; in other cas-es, it realizes a 'neo-Taylorist' NPM that implies the bureau-cratization of profes-sional work and a gradual reduction in the autonomy and discretion of profes-sionals. | - |
| Kirkpatrick and Ackroyd (2003) | Health and social care | UK | Professional models, despite calling for changes, produced a resistance to change processes to maintain the *status quo*. | Radical shifts in arche-types, following new management practices. |
| Kitchener and Gask (2003) | Health and social care | Wales | NPM provides no more of a panacea for poor service co-ordination than do professional struc-tures or markets. | - |
| Knott (2011) | - | USA | Bureaucracy produc-es rent seeking, cor-ruption, repression of minorities, and moral hazard. | Credibility requires pro-fessional public agencies that operate within the broad framework of democratic accountabil-ity. |
| Knott and Miller (2006) | N/A | UK and USA | The design of previ-ous public models led political elites to engage in corruption and extracting rents from the economy. | Principal agent theory and the NPM favor greater accountability of public managers to elected offi-cials. |

*see next page*

| Learmonth (2005) | Health and social care | UK | Use of the words "management" and "administration" without distinction suggests a dominance that has come to favor the interests of some as it denies the interests of others. | - |
|---|---|---|---|---|
| Lynn (2001) | Central government | - | Bureaucracy has turned out to be both the solution and the problem, an apparatus that provides structure and continuity to modern states but, at the same time, poses a threat to democratic and party control. | Need to emphasize the importance of better national and comparative evidence on administrative and managerial change. |
| Meyer et al. (2014) | Local government | Austria | The Weberian legalistic-bureaucratic logic supports neither a high attraction to policy-making nor a high level of compassion. | A managerial orientation entails significantly higher scores on these two dimensions, as well as on overall public service motivation. |
| Noordegraaf and Abma (2003) | - | - | In the search for transparency and effectiveness, NPM introduces standardized cycles to measure performance that lead to interpretive spaces. | Management and measurement in the public sphere must be contextualized and such a contextual-ization inevitably leads to an interweaving of fact and value. |
| Noordegraaf and De Wit (2012) | Education | The Netherlands | Management reforms drive public and non-profit managers away from professionals on work floors by increasing clashes between them. | Individuals, especially professionals, must find individual solutions to cope with issues related to the managerial-ization of public services. |

The NPM approach strongly criticizes previous models by arguing that, despite calling for change, they always produced a resistance to change processes to maintain the *status quo* (Kickert, 2011; Kirkpatrick and Ackroyd, 2003), thus remaining inflexible and impersonal (Charlesworth et al., 1996), becoming a threat to democratic control (Lynn, 2001), and leading to phenomena such as corruption and rent-seeking (Knott, 2011; Knott and Miller, 2006).

According to the authors that espouse the NPM approach, radical shifts in organizational archetypes should arise following new management practices (Kirkpatrick and Ackroyd, 2003; Noordegraaf and De Wit, 2012) that are customer-centered (Charlesworth et al., 1996), to increase accountability, transparence, flexibility (Ahn and Bretschneider, 2011; Charlesworth et al., 1996; Kickert, 2005; Knott, 2011; Knott and Miller, 2006), and public service motivation (Meyer et al., 2014).

## 6.5. The New Public Governance and the collaborative/representative approach

Literature started considering the New Public Governance approach around the year 2006, after more than a decade of contrasting results emerging from the application of NPM principles. The concepts that formed the basis for the new approach are related to themes such as collaboration, participation, and stakeholders' involvement. The reasons underlying the change are that NPM lacked representativeness and involvement of public stakeholders in the decision-making process.

Results from this review show that some papers which may fall within this category were published before 2005, even if the critical mass of contributions can be found after the year 2008.

**Table 1.10.** Studies focusing on New Public Governance and collaborative/representative approaches.

| Authors | PA observed | Country | Critiques of other models/approaches | Main proposals |
|---|---|---|---|---|
| Bevir and Richards (2009) | - | - | The analysis of policy networks lacks a view on the "micro" dimension. | A decentered approach to networks offers a micro-theory based on individuals acting in accordance with beliefs and desires forged against the background of specific traditions and dilemmas. |
| Callanan (2005) | Local government | Ireland | - | Participative structures of governance enhance representative and participatory democracy. |
| Carey and Matthews (2017) | Health and social care | Australia | One weakness of the NPM is that it has framed cost effectiveness and productivity in the public sector simplistically; NPG introduced the concept of flexible networks, but still maintaining several concepts of NPM. | Governments should develop greater openness to risk and policy experimentation during implementation. |

*see next page*

| | | | | |
|---|---|---|---|---|
| Currie et al. (2011) | Local government | England | Lack of effectiveness and efficiency in public service delivery. | Networks and distributed leadership to ensure more efficient integration of services, tackling complex problems, organizational learning, and innovation, or mediating the democratic deficit. |
| Entwistle and Martin (2005) | Local government | UK | Dissatisfaction and short-term, low-trust relationships between principals and agents. | Create partnerships to encourage trust, reduce conflict in relational exchange, and deliver a transformational approach to service improvement. |
| Geddes (2012) | Local government | England | - | Develop a collaborative public governance. |
| Jeffares and Skelcher (2011) | - | England, Netherlands | - | Network forms of governance enhance positive interactions with citizens, civil society organizations, and businesses, and configure democratic legitimacy and accountability. |
| Kelly (2006) | Central government | UK | - | The action of central government is guaranteed and sustained by its participation in vertical and horizontal networks and partnerships with practitioners from local government institutions who form part of local governance arrangements. |
| Martin (2011) | Health and social care | UK | Previous models highlighted the lack of top-down support for a more influential model of users' involvement. | A more inclusive governance network. |
| Martin et al. (2009) | Health and social care | England | Bureaucracy and professional bureaucracy are characterized by looseness of accountability and practitioner autonomy. | Networks and distributed leadership may lead to effective collaboration and establishment of reforms through structural integration and the harnessing of agency. |
| Meier and Bohte (2001) | Education | USA (Texas) | Representative bureaucracy suffers limitations such as organizational socialization, structured jobs, lack of relevant decisions, location in the hierarchy, and legal constraints. | New models of representative bureaucracy must consider active representation by developing policy discretion and using less rigid control. |

*see next page*

| Meynhardt and Diefen- bach (2012) | Federal labor agency | Germany | Bureaucracy leads to inflexible structures, indifferent and bureau- cratic staff, and overall unsatisfying perfor- mance; NPM narrowly focuses on measurable performance and short- term orientation. | Develop an entrepreneurial orientation for public value creation which emphasizes context variables such as culture, regulatory struc- tures, as well as cognitive factors. |
|---|---|---|---|---|
| Ongaro (2006) | Local government | Italy (Lombardy) | The administrative law paradigm operates to impede, or at least slow down, the implementa- tion process of devolu- tion reforms. | Some key facts are found to solve highlighted problems: the way top managers are selected and incentivized; the way the reallocation of per- sonnel is managed; and the way the engagement of key social groups is conducted. |
| Raadschel ders (1995) | Local government | Netherlands | Classic models of pub- lic governance highlight a lack of reciprocity between government and citizen. | Citizens' involvement may well lead to different solu- tions to current government problems. |
| Seibel (2010) | - | Germany | Bureaucracy receives pressing issues on per- formance and control for the sake of account- ability and policy out- come improvement. It does not conform to the standard model of dem- ocratic integration through parties, civil society, and parliaments. | A non-hierarchical, non- legalistic, semi-professional, decentralized, and adaptive public administration, prone to building compro- mises and cooperative rela- tionships with societal groups. However, this mod- el depends on the quality of the represented groups. |
| Shaw (2013) | - | - | Public value manage- ment has not solved all the issues emerging from NPM: rent-seeking be- haviors, instrumentality, lack of accountability, and lack of public stake- holder involvement. | More decision-making au- tonomy for public Manag- ers, and greater civil society involvement in that deci- sion-making, are realized. |
| Sorensen and Torf- ing (2009) | - | - | Discrepancy between the steadily rising steer- ing ambitions and the increasing fragmenta- tion of social and polit- ical life. | Enhance democratic partic- ipation in public policy- making through the estab- lishment of governance networks (public and pri- vate actors). |
| Voets et al. (2015) | Health and social care | Belgium | Hierarchy and bureau- cracy lead governments to act unilaterally with- out stakeholder partici- pation or consultation, risking ineffectiveness. | A collaborative approach allows a coordination that ensures organizations work together and help clients (citizens) to navigate clearly through the complex field of public organizations. |

*see next page*

| Williams et al. (2016) | Health and social care | USA, South Korea | Existing approaches show a lack of account-ability, insufficient training, or lax legal standards that arise from simple user partic-ipation. Additional bar-riers due to user-led innovation include re-sistance from service providers to cede au-thority or inefficiency due to service fragmen-tation. | New approaches should address user involvement at both the strategic and oper-ational levels for the devel-opment and implementation of public services. |
|---|---|---|---|---|

Authors espousing the NPG approach accuse the NPM approach of short-term orientation, rent-seeking, having a narrow focus on measurable performance (Entwistle and Martin, 2005; Meynhardt and Diefenbach, 2012; Shaw, 2013), lack of representativeness and user involvement (Martin, 2011), and lack of consideration toward culture and cognitive factors (Meynhardt and Diefenbach, 2012). Indeed, Carey and Matthews (2017) accuse the NPM approach of having simplistically framed cost effectiveness and productivity in the public sector without contextualizing its application.

Other authors (Currie et al., 2011; Martin et al., 2009; Williams et al., 2016) criticize the bureaucratic approach with regard to the lack of effectiveness and efficiency in public service delivery, looseness of accountability, and practitioner autonomy.

According to the authors, solutions might be found in enhancing collaboration, democratic participation, and civil society involvement (Callanan, 2005; Entwistle and Martin, 2005; Geddes, 2012; Jeffares and Skelcher, 2011; Kelly, 2006; Seibel, 2010; Shaw, 2013; Sorensen and Torfing, 2009; Voets et al., 2015; Williams et al., 2016), and developing distributed leadership (Currie et al., 2011; Martin et al., 2009).

## 6.6. Hybrid models

The label "hybrid models" refers to those models developed by merging different arrangements: some authors consider hybrid forms of public administration to be arrangements between markets, collaboration, and steering; in other cases, hybridized forms combine traditional bureaucracy with increased flexibility and user focus.

Contributions within this category, with exception of two works (2004 and 2006), have been mainly published after the year 2010.

**Table 1.11.** Studies focusing on hybrid models.

| Authors | PA observed | Country | Critiques of other models/approaches | Main proposals |
|---|---|---|---|---|
| Bang (2004) | Local government | Denmark | Bureaucracy is far from being modern and representative; it is also unable to meet the complexity of tasks. | The solution should neither be hierarchical nor bureaucratic, but empowering and self-disciplining. It manifests itself as various forms of joined-up government and network governance, and proclaims itself as genuinely democratic and dialogical. |
| Berg (2006) | N/A | Norway | NPM reforms led professionals in the public sector to resist change due to its challenge to their culture and identity. | Develop a hybrid form that combines traditional procedural bureaucracy with flexibility, user focus, participation, and professional pride. |
| Bode and Dent (2014) | Health and social care | Europe | The advent of NPM led to a shift from a professional culture to a managerial one; this led to the risk of seeing medical orientation crowded out by a technocratic and business-like management approach; professional autonomy is challenged by NPM reforms. | Developing a hybrid professionalism based on incentives should solve the problem to let clinicians, as professionals, enter managerial roles. |
| Correia and Denis (2016) | Health and social care | Portugal | Professional autonomy in hospitals (alike professional bureaucracy) is limited by classic bureaucratic managers. | Including hybrid managers (professionals) in the directorate leads medicals to an increased autonomy and to be more accountable to managerial criteria. |
| Denis et al. (2015) | N/A | N/A | NPM does not engage with civil society. | A broader approach to hybridity that pays attention to structures, institutional dynamics, social interactions, and new identities and roles. |
| Dwyer (2010) | Health and social care | N/A | - | Embrace (medical) professionals in key managerial and leadership roles. |
| Fotaki (2011) | Health and social care | England and Sweden | Pro-market policies are likely to promote a new type of highly volatile and fragile partnership. | Adopting new hybrid arrangements between markets, collaboration, and steering. |

*see next page*

| Gatenby et al. (2014) | Local government, health and social care | UK | Bureaucracy restricts the flow of knowledge and communication across the organization; instances of professional 'hybridity' have not led to convincing changes; NPM principles of flexibility and decentralized structures are merely 'illusory'. | - |
|---|---|---|---|---|
| McGivern et al. (2015) | Health and social care | UK | The NPM accent on performance and efficiency challenges the professional autonomy within professional bureaucracies. | Hybridization is the response to maintain the professional identity and wider professionalism in organizational and policy contexts affected by managerialist ideas. |
| Skelcher and Smith (2015) | N/A | N/A | - | Hybrid forms are more likely to respond to institutional logics. Hybridization is a process in which plural logics – and thus actor identities – are in play within an organization, leading to a number of possible improved outcomes. |

The main criticisms applied to previous models are that bureaucracy is far from being modern and representative and that it is also unable to meet the complexity of tasks (Bang, 2004). Indeed, the NPM does not engage with civil society (Denis et al., 2015): its reforms lead professionals in the public sector to resist change due to its challenge of professionals' culture and identity (Berg, 2006; Bode and Dent, 2014; Correia and Denis, 2016; McGivern et al., 2015). Additionally, NPM pro-market policies, instead of meeting the alleged needs of post-modern users for individualized public services, are likely to promote a new type of highly volatile and fragile partnership, and create a new subordinated user who has no choice but to 'choose' services (Fotaki, 2011). Furthermore, NPM principles of flexibility and decentralized structure are merely illusory (Gatenby et al., 2014).

Solutions proposed by authors significantly differ in terms of whether they concentrate on the internal organizational structure or on the best structure to co-operate with external actors. For instance, some authors (Denis et al., 2015; Bang, 2004; Berg, 2006; Fotaki, 2011) concentrate on the fact that public organizations should not adopt hierarchical or bureaucratic forms, but rather joined-up forms of government and network governance, to be genuinely democratic and dialogical. In particular, Denis et al. (2015) assert that the approach to hybridity should pay attention to structures, institutional dynamics, social interactions, and new identities and roles, while Berg (2006) suggests developing a hybrid form that combines the traditional procedural bureaucracy with flexibility, user focus, participation, and professional pride. Other authors (Bode and Dent, 2014; Correia and Denis, 2016; Dwyer, 2010) concentrate more on internal aspects related to considering professionals in key managerial and leadership roles and to increase their autonomy, so that they would be more accountable to managerial criteria.

## 6.7. The behavioral approach

A behavioral approach has been found in only three papers. Such an approach is based on the analysis of those factors and dimensions that influence the dynamics of interaction among individuals and this interaction influences individuals' behaviors. Two of these papers were published in 2005 and 2006, and one in 2010.

**Table 1.12.** Studies concerning the behavioral approach.

| Authors | PA observed | Country | Critiques of other models/approaches | Main proposals |
|---|---|---|---|---|
| Currie and Procter (2005) | Healthcare | UK | The drive for efficiency led by NPM has combined with downsizing and decentralization to the disadvantage of middle managers, because they have been delayered. | Paying attention to socialization processes, identity, and personal characteristics. |
| Finn et al. (2010) | Healthcare | UK | Professional bureaucracies rely on a willingness and ability to both cede power and take it on. | Encouraging team work, establishing a distributed leadership, focusing on human and social dimensions, paying attention to role and career expectations, skills and experience, and working relationships between members. |
| Nielsen (2006) | Local government | Denmark | Public employees' negative behaviors engendered by bureaucracy lead to a negative relationship with clients. | Looking at the interests that motivate the bureaucrat and the characteristics of the relationship between the bureaucrat and the client allows a better understanding of his or her behavior. |

Currie and Procter (2005) criticize the NPM approach as its drive for efficiency has led to a process of downsizing and de-layering of middle managers. The role conflict and ambiguity suffered by middle managers that results from this situation may be resolved by paying more attention to socialization processes, and considering managers' identity and personal characteristics.

Finn et al. (2010) argue that bureaucracies and professional bureaucracies rely on a willingness and ability to both cede power and take it on, while the attention should be moved toward encouraging team work, with a distributed leadership, and focusing on human and social dimensions, paying attention to role and career expectations, skills, and experience, and working relationships between members. Indeed, Nielsen (2006) asserts that bureaucracy has led public employees to assume negative behaviors that, in turn, worsen the relationship with clients. A solution to avoid these behaviors may be found in widening both the range of interests that motivate the bureaucrat and the characteristics of the relationship between the street-level bureaucrat and the client: we get a more nuanced and plausible picture of the positive and negative pressures of the job a street-level bureaucrat might put on the bureaucrat and therefore a better understanding of his or her behavior.

## 6.8. A chronological allocation of contributions

Aiming to clarify the chronological allocation of contributions, the following Figure 1.2 reproduces the contributions on a timeline. This image enables us to make some in-depth considerations on the main trends within literature.

**Figure 1.2.** Time allocation of contributions.

*Notes:* PB = professional bureaucracy; BH = behavioral approach.

As can be seen, the NPM approach covers the whole period observed, while the NPG approach (along with collaborative and representative approaches) starts from 2005; other approaches such as classic and reflexive bureaucracy cover just a few years (respectively 2006-2009 and 2009-2012), representing small parentheses in the observed period.

The hybrid approach starts from 2010 and seems to be the bigger trend in recent years. This is also confirmed by the correlation test (see Table 1.5) that shows a positive correlation between year and hybrid approach (0.294 with $p < 0.05$).

## 7. Discussion

The analyzed literature provides interesting critiques of all the models/approaches, as well as interesting solutions to be adopted to improve these models. For instance, Kickert (2011) interestingly summarizes the main criticisms of all the public administration models. According to the author, bureaucracy is characterized by immobilism and inertia, formalism, clientelism, patronage, and corruption; NPM reforms led to very small changes, and with NPG no substantial changes occurred in respect of the NPM approach. In terms of solutions to be adopted, academics have provided interesting suggestions – for instance, in relation to good managerial practices, flexible models, professionals' autonomy, and the engagement of civil society.

However, two important gaps emerge from the analysis. Firstly, there is a lack of attention toward individuals and their behaviors within public organizations. Also, greater attention has been paid to Anglo-Saxon countries, while Continental European countries – especially those in the Southern area – are still under-investigated despite their peculiarities, in terms of cultural, political, and economic characteristics.

In fact, both academics focusing on internal issues and academics focusing on external issues concerning the public organization put the accent mainly on structural aspects. For instance, aspects analyzed concern hierarchy, management practices, the involvement of professionals in the directorate, the adoption of flexible models, the establishment of external networks, the adoption of hybrid forms, the involvement of external actors, etc.

Even if these aspects are key to setting up important processes of organizational change, they represent only a part of the more complex issue regarding the public sector. In fact, since organizations are basically made of individuals, and since main criticisms of bureaucratic models are related to negative individual behaviors such as episodes of corruption, rent-seeking, and opportunism, a strong lack of attention emerges toward individuals and their behaviors. Some academics (e.g., Knott and Miller, 2006) argue here that, since public models lead political elites to engage in corruption and extracting rents, increased levels of transparency, professionalism, and legality should help ensuring that public managers do not engage in these negative behaviors. On these grounds, in fact, it is worth noting that effective processes of change may occur only when they also involve aspects such as organizational culture and individuals' behaviors.

As previously highlighted, only three papers emerging from the literature review use a behavioral approach, analyzing the importance of interactions and socialization processes, personal identity and characteristics, personal experiences, and issues regarding role conflict and ambiguity.

It is in fact true that, by adopting a mainstream approach, most of the analyzed papers take for granted the logics of power and politics and never focus on the importance of culture, context, and complexity.

Additionally, the lack of attention afforded to individuals' behaviors is confirmed by counting the use of the words "behavior" (or "behaviour") and "behavioral" (or "behavioural") within papers. With the exception of the three papers falling in the behavioral approach category, 50 papers out of 65 cite the words "behavior" or "behavioral", with a total of 326 citations: on average, each paper cites the word "behavior" 6.5 times. This information taken alone does not convey any particular meaning, but it assumes greater importance if linked to the fact that, within these papers, the word "behavior" never means to discuss issues concerning individuals' behaviors. Even when authors recognize this issue, the solutions advanced to the problems within public administrations are not related to behavioral issues.

Thus, new models for public administrations should be developed by paying increased attention to individual interaction, group dynamics, leadership, and the development of other soft skills for public managers useful to enhance positive individual behaviors, and to manage people and activities properly in a highly standardized context such as the public.

On this basis, the second chapter problematizes public sector management from the perspective of the behavioral approach. Firstly, the chapter addresses the debate on the behavioral approach and its importance, building on literature based in the for-profit sector. Then it deepens these issues, showing the main implications for the public sector. In the end, building on previous content and moving on from the framework advanced by Huse (2007), it builds an adapted theoretical framework for studying and analyzing the behavioral approach within public administrations.

The third chapter will aim to fill the gap in literature regarding the attention paid to Continental European countries – especially those in the Southern area – by carrying out an analysis in the Italian context, on the grounds of its peculiar political, cultural, and contextual aspects. The analysis will rely upon a mixed methods approach, using both questionnaires administered to 156 Italian public managers, officers, and employees, and face-to-face interviews to better catch the nuances emerging from participants' replies to the questionnaire.

Some limitations of the systematic literature review presented in this chapter may result from the selection criteria both of keywords and of relevant studies. One of the main limitations of a literature review is in fact generally recognized to be the possible subjective bias in the choice of keywords and in the following criteria for discarding non- relevant papers or selecting those perceived to be relevant.

Even in acknowledging this limitation, it is worth noting that in this chapter the aim was to raise awareness about issues and limitations surrounding the bureaucratic model, and consequently to individuate the main post-bureaucratic models discussed in literature. Additionally, some critiques of post-bureaucratic models emerged, thus enabling further discussion of what might be a step forward in the analysis of the public sector.

## 8. References

Ahn M.J., and Bretschneider S. (2011), Politics of E-Government: E-Government and the Political Control of Bureaucracy, *Public Administration Review*, vol. 71, no. 3, pp. 414-424. doi: 10.1111/j.1540-6210.2011.02225.x.

Alexander D., Lewis J.M., and Considine M. (2011), How Politicians and Bureaucrats Network: A Comparison Across Governments, *Public Administration*, vol. 89, no. 4, pp. 1274-1292. doi: 10.1111/j.1467-9299.2010.01890.x.

Bang H.P. (2004), Culture Governance: Governing Self-Reflexive Modernity, *Public Administration*, vol. 82, no. 1, pp. 157-190, doi: 10.1111/j.0033-3298.2004.00389.x.

Berg A.M. (2006), Transforming public services – transforming the public servant?, *International Journal of Public Sector Management*, vol. 19, no. 6, pp. 556-568, doi: 10.1108/09513550610686627.

Bevir M., and Richards D., (2009), Decentring Policy Networks: Lessons And Prospects, *Public Administration*, Vol. 87, no. 1, pp. 132-141, DOI: 10.1111/j.1467-9299.2008.01739.x.

Blau P.M., (1955), *The dynamics of bureaucracy: a study of interpersonal relations in two Government Agencies*, Chicago: University of Chicago Press.

Bode I., and Dent M. (2014), Converging hybrid worlds? Medicine and hospital management in Europe, *International Journal of Public Sector Management*, vol. 27, no. 5, doi: 10.1108/IJPSM-01-2013-0011.

Bouckaert, G., and Balk, W., (1991), Public productivity measurement: diseases and cures, *Public Productivity & Management Review*, vol. 15, no. 2, pp. 229-235. DOI: 10.2307/3380763.

Callanan M. (2005), Institutionalizing Participation and Governance? New Partici-pative Structures in Local Government in Ireland, *Public Administration*, vol. 83, no. 4, pp. 909-929. doi: 10.1111/j.0033-3298.2005.00483.x.

Carey G., and Matthews M. (2017), Methods for Delivering Complex Social Ser-vices: Exploring adaptive management and regulation in the Australian national disability insurance scheme, *Public Management Review*, vol. 19, no. 2, pp. 194-211, doi:10.1080/14719037.2016.1148194.

Chalkley, M., Tilley, C., Young, L., Bonetti, D., and Clarkson, J. (2010), Incentives for dentists in public service: evidence from a natural experiment, *Journal of Public Administration Research and Theory*, vol. 20, SI 2, pp. 207-223. Doi: 10.1093/jopart/muq025.

Charlesworth J., Clarke J., and Cochrane A. (1996), Tangled Webs? Managing Lo-cal Mixed Economies Of Care, *Public Administration*, vol. 74, no. 1, pp. 67-88, doi: 10.1111/j.1467-9299.1996.tb00858.x.

Chris Skelcher And Steven Rathgeb Smith, (2015), Theorizing Hybridity: Institutional Logics, Complex Organizations, And Actor Identities: The Case Of Nonprofits, *Public Administration*, Vol. 93, no. 2, pp. 433-448, doi: 10.1111/padm.12105.

Considine M. (2000), Contract Regimes and Reflexive Governance: Comparing Employment Service Reforms in the United Kingdom, the Netherlands, New Zealand and Australia, *Public Administration*, vol. 78, no. 3, pp. 613-638, doi: 10.1111/1467-9299.00221.

Correia, T., and Denis, J.L. (2016), Hybrid management, organizational configura-tion, and medical professionalism: evidence from the establishment of a clinical directorate in Portugal, *BMC Health Services Research*, vol. 16, SI 2, pp. 161-171, doi: 10.1186/s12913-016-1398-2.

Currie, G., and Procter, S.J. (2005), The antecedents of middle managers' strategic contribution: The case of a professional bureaucracy, *Journal Of Management Studies*, vol. 42, no. 7, pp. 1325-1356, doi: 10.1111/j.1467-6486.2005.00546.x.

Currie G., Grubnic S., and Hodges R. (2011), Leadership In Public Services Net-works: Antecedents, Process And Outcome, *Public Administration*, vol. 89, no. 2, pp. 242-264, doi: 10.1111/J.1467-9299.2011.01931.X.

De Boer H.F., Enders J., and Leisyte L. (2007), Public Sector Reform In Dutch Higher Education: The Organizational Transformation Of The University, *Public Admin-istration*, vol. 85, no. 1, pp. 27-46, doi: 10.1111/j.1467-9299.2007.00632.x.

Denis J.L., Ferlie E., and Van Gestel N., (2015), Understanding Hybridity In Pub-lic Organizations, *Public Administration*, Vol. 93, no. 2, pp. 273-289, doi: 10.1111/padm.12175.

Dunleavy, P., and Hood, C., (1994), From old public administration to new public management, *Public Money and Management*, vol. 14, no. 3, pp. 9-16. Doi: 10.1080/09540969409387823.

Dunleavy, P., Margetts, H., Bastow, S. and Tinkler, J. (2006), New Public Management is dead. Long live digital-era governance, *Journal of Public Administration Research and Theory*, vol. 16, no. 3, pp. 467-494. Doi: 10.1093/jopart/mui057.

Dwyer, A.J., (2010), Medical managers in contemporary healthcare organisations: a consideration of the literature, *Australian Health Review*, vol. 34, no. 4, pp. 514-522, doi: 10.1071/AH09736.

Entwistle T., and Martin S. (2005), From Competition to Collaboration in Public Service Delivery: A New Agenda for Research, *Public Administration*, vol. 83, no. 1, pp. 233-242, doi: 10.1111/j.0033-3298.2005.00446.x.

Esmark A., (2009), The Functional Differentiation Of Governance: Public Governance Beyond Hierarchy, Market And Networks, *Public Administration*, Vol. 87, no. 2, pp. 351–370, DOI: 10.1111/j.1467-9299.2009.01759.x.

Finn, R., Currie, G., and Martin G. (2010), Team Work in Context: Institutional Mediation in the Public-service Professional Bureaucracy, *Organization Studies*, vol. 31, no. 8, pp. 1069-1097, doi: 10.1177/0170840610376142.

Fotaki M. (2011), Towards Developing New Partnerships In Public Services: Users As Consumers, Citizens And/Or Co-Producers In Health And Social Care In England And Sweden, *Public Administration*, vol. 89, no. 3, pp. 933-955, doi: 10.1111/j.1467-9299.2010.01879.x.

Gatenby M., Rees C., Truss C., Alfes K., and Soane E. (2015), Managing Change, or Changing Managers? The role of middle managers in UK public service reform, *Public Management Review*, vol. 17, no. 8, pp. 1124-1145, doi: 10.1080/14719037.2014.895028.

Geddes L., (2012), In Search of Collaborative Public Management, *Public Management Review*, vol. 14, no. 7, pp. 947-966, doi: 10.1080/14719037.2011.650057.

Germov, J. (2005), Managerialism in the Australian public health sector: towards the hyper-rationalisation of professional bureaucracies, *Sociology Of Health & Illness*, vol. 27, no. 6, pp. 738-758, doi: 10.1111/j.1467-9566.2005.00472.x.

Gourdin, G., and Schepers, R. (2009), Hospital governance and the medical practitioner in Belgium, *Journal Of Health Organization And Management*, vol. 23, no. 3, pp. 319-331, doi: 10.1108/14777260910966744.

Hammerschmid G., and Meyer R.E. (2005), New Public Management in Austria: Local Variation on a Global Theme?, *Public Administration*, vol. 83, no. 3, pp. 709-733, doi: 10.1111/j.0033-3298.2005.00471.x.

Haynes P. (2015), *Managing Complexity in the Public Services* (2nd edition), London: Routledge.

Hood C. (1991), A Public Management for all Seasons?, *Public Administration*, vol. 69, no. 1, pp. 3-39. doi: 10.1111/j.1467-9299.1991.tb00778.x.

Hood, C., and Peters, G. (2004) The middle aging of new public management: into the age of paradox?, *Journal of Public Administration Research and Theory*, vol. 14, no. 3, pp. 267-282. Doi: 10.1093/jopart/muh019.

Houston, D., (2000), Public service motivation: a multivariate test, *Journal of Public Administration Research and Theory*, vol. 10, no. 4, pp. 713-728. Doi: 10.1093/oxfordjournals.jpart.a024288.

Jeffares S., and Skelcher C. (2011), Democratic Subjectivities In Network Governance: A Q Methodology Study Of English And Dutch Public Managers, *Public Administration*, vol. 89, no. 4, pp. 1253–1273, doi: 10.1111/j.1467-9299.2010.01888.x.

Kale P., Singh H., (2007). Building Firm Capabilities Through Learning: The Role Of The Alliance Learning Process In Alliance Capability And Firm-Level Alliance Success, *Strategic Management Journal*, vol. 28, n. 10, pp. 981-1000. Doi: 10.1002/smj.616.

Kane J., and Patapan H. (2006), In Search of Prudence: The Hidden Problem of Managerial Reform, *Public Administration Review*, vol. 66, no. 5, pp. 711-724, doi: 10.1111/j.1540-6210.2006.00636.x.

Kelly J. (2006), Central Regulation Of English Local Authorities: An Example Of Meta-Governance?, *Public Administration*, vol. 84, no. 3, pp. 603-621, doi: 10.1111/j.1467-9299.2006.00604.x.

Kettl, D. (1997), The global revolution in public management: driving themes, missing links, *Journal of Policy Analysis and Management*, vol.16, no.3, pp. 446-462. Doi: 10.1002/(SICI)1520-6688(199722)16:3<446::AID-PAM5>3.0.CO;2-H.

Khan K.S., Kunz R., Kleijnen J., and Antes G., (2003), Five steps to conducting a systematic review, *Journal of the Royal Society of Medicine*, vol. 96, no. 3, pp. 118-121. PMCID: PMC539417.

Kickert W.J.M. (2005), Distinctiveness in the study of public management in Europe, *Public Management Review*, vol. 7, no. 4, pp. 537-563, doi: 10.1080/14719030500362470.

Kickert W.J.M. (2011), Distinctiveness Of Administrative Reform In Greece, Italy, Portugal And Spain. Common Characteristics Of Context, Administrations And Reforms, *Public Administration,* vol. 89, no. 3, pp. 801-818. doi: 10.1111/j.1467-9299.2010.01862.x.

Kinder T. (2012), Learning, Innovating and Performance in Post-New Public Management of Locally Delivered Public Services, *Public Management Review*, vol. 14, no. 3, pp. 403-428, doi: 10.1080/14719037.2011.637408.

Kirkpatrick I. (1999), Managers or Colleagues?, *Public Management: An International Journal of Research and Theory*, vol. 1, no. 4, pp. 489-509, doi: 10.1080/14719039900000023.

Kirkpatrick I., and Ackroyd S. (2003), Transforming the professional archetype?, *Public Management Review*, vol. 5, no. 4, pp. 509-529. doi: 10.1080/1471903032000178563.

Kitchener M., and Gask L. (2003), NPM merger mania. Lessons from an early case, *Public Management Review*, vol. 5, no. 1, pp. 19-44. doi: 10.1080/1461667022000028843.

Klijn, E.H. (2008), Complexity theory and Public Administration: what's new? Key concepts in complexity theory compared to their counterparts in public administration, *Public Management Review*, vol. 10, n. 3, pp. 299-317. doi: 10.1080/14719030802002675.

Knott J.H., Miller G.J. (2006), Social welfare, corruption and credibility, *Public Management Review*, vol. 8, no. 2, pp. 227-252, doi: 10.1080/14719030600587455.

Knott J.H. (2011), Federalist No. 10: Are Factions the Problem in Creating Democratic Accountability in the Public Interest?, *Public Administration Review*, vol. 71, SI 1, pp. s29-s36, doi: 10.1111/j.1540-6210.2011.02459.x.

Kooiman J., Jentoft S. (2009), Meta-governance: values, norms and principles, and the making of hard choices, *Public Administration*, vol. 87, no. 4, pp. 818-836. doi: 10.1111/j.1467-9299.2009.01780.x.

Kothari, S., and Handscombe, R.D. (2007), Sweep or seep? Structure, culture, enterprise and universities, *Management Decision*, vol. 45, no. 1, pp. 43-61, doi: 10.1108/00251740710718953.

Lapsley I. (2008), The NPM Agenda: back to the future, *Financial Accountability & Management*, vol. 24, no. 1, pp. 77-96. doi: 10.1111/j.1468-0408.2008.00444.x.

Lapsley I. (2009), New Public Management: The Cruellest Invention of the Human Spirit?, *ABACUS*, vol. 45, no. 1, pp. 1-21. doi: 10.1111/j.1467-6281.2009.00275.x.

Learmonth M. 2005. "Doing Things with Words: The Case of 'Management' and 'Administration'." *Public Administration* 83 (3): 617-637. doi: 10.1111/j.0033-3298.2005.00465.x.

Lega, F., and DePietro, C. (2005), Converging patterns in hospital organization: beyond the professional bureaucracy, *Health Policy*, vol. 74, no. 3, pp. 261-281, doi: 10.1016/j.healthpol.2005.01.010.

Luhmann N., (1995), *Social Systems*, Stanford: Stanford University Press.

Lynn L.E., (2001), Globalization And Administrative Reform: – What is happening in theory?, *Public Management Review*, Vol. 3, no. 2, pp. 191-208. doi: 10.1080/14616670010029584.

Magone J.M. (2011), The Difficult Transformation Of State And Public Administration In Portugal. Europeanization And The Persistence Of Neo-Patrimonialism, *Public Administration*, vol. 89, no. 3, pp. 756-782, doi: 10.1111/j.1467-9299.2011.01913.x.

Maguire S., and McKelvey B., (1999), Special Issue on Complexity and Management: Where Are We, *Emergence: Complexity and Organization*, vol. 1, no. 2, pp. 19-61.

Martin G.P. (2011), The Third Sector, User Involvement And Public Service Reform: A Case Study In The Co-Governance Of Health Service Provision, *Public Administration*, vol. 89, no. 3, pp. 909-932, doi: 10.1111/j.1467-9299.2011.01910.x.

Martin G.P., Currie G., and Finn R. (2009), Leadership, Service Reform, and Public-Service Networks: The Case of Cancer-Genetics Pilots in the English NHS, *Journal of Public Administration Research and Theory*, vol. 19, no. 4, pp. 769-794, doi:10.1093/jopart/mun016.

McFarland A., (1969), *Power and leadership in pluralist systems*, Palo Alto: Stanford University Press.

McGivern G., Currie G., Ferlie E., Fitzgerald L., and Waring J. (2015), Hybrid Manager-Professionals' Identity Work: The Maintenance And Hybridization Of Medical Professionalism In Managerial Contexts, *Public Administration*, vol. 93, no. 2, pp. 412-432, doi: 10.1111/padm.12119.

Meadows D., (2009), *Thinking in systems: A Primer*, London: Earthscan.

Meek J.W., (2010), Complexity Theory for Public Administration and Policy, *Emergence: Complexity & Organization*, vol. 12, n. 1, pp. 1-4.

Meier K.J., and Bohte J. (2001), Structure and Discretion: Missing Links in Representative Bureaucracy, *Journal of Public Administration Research and Theory*, vol. 11, no. 4, pp. 455-470, doi: 10.1093/oxfordjournals.jpart.a003511.

Mengistu B., and Vogel E., (2006), Bureaucratic Neutrality among Competing Bureaucratic Values in an Ethnic Federalism: The Case of Ethiopia, *Public Administration Review*, Vol. 66, no. 2, pp. 205-216. Doi: 10.1111/j.1540-6210.2006.00573.x.

Merton R.K., (1940), Bureaucratic Structure and Personality, *Social Forces*, vol. 18, n. 4, pp. 560-568. doi: 10.2307/2570634.

Meyer R.E., Egger-Peitler I., Höllerer M.A., Hammerschmid G. (2014), Of Bureaucrats And Passionate Public Managers: Institutional Logics, Executive Identities, And Public Service Motivation, *Public Administration*, vol. 92, no. 4, pp. 861-885, doi: 10.1111/j.1467-9299.2012.02105.x.

Meynhardt T., and Diefenbach F. E. (2012), What Drives Entrepreneurial Orientation in the Public Sector? Evidence from Germany's Federal Labor Agency, *Journal of Public Administration Research and Theory*, vol. 22, no. 4, pp. 761-792, doi:10.1093/jopart/mus013.

Mintzberg, H. (1979), *The Structuring of Organizations*, Englewood Cliffs: Prentice Hall.

Nielsen V.L. (2006), Are Street-Level Bureaucrats Compelled Or Enticed To Cope?, *Public Administration*, vol. 84, no. 4, pp. 861-889, doi: 10.1111/j.1467-9299.2006.00616.x.

Nonaka I., (1994), A dynamic theory of organizational knowledge creation, *Organization Science*, vol. 5, n. 1, pp. 14-37. Doi: 10.1287/orsc.5.1.14.

Noordegraaf M., and Abma T. (2003), Management by Measurement? Public Management Practices Amidst Ambiguity, *Public Administration*, vol. 81, no. 4, pp. 853-871, doi: 10.1111/j.0033-3298.2003.00374.x.

Noordegraaf M., and De Wit B. (2012), Responses To Managerialism: How Management Pressures Affect Managerial Relations And Loyalties In Education, *Public Administration*, vol. 90, no. 4, pp. 957-973, doi: 10.1111/j.1467-9299.2012.02068.x.

Ongaro E. (2006), The Dynamics Of Devolution Processes In Legalistic Countries: Organizational Change In The Italian Public Sector, *Public Administration*, vol. 84, no. 3, pp. 737-770, doi: 10.1111/j.1467-9299.2006.00610.x.

Orr K., and Vince R. (2009), Traditions Of Local Government, *Public Administration*, vol. 87, no. 3, pp. 655-677, doi: 10.1111/j.1467-9299.2009.01770.x.

Osborne S.P. (2006), The New Public Governance?, *Public Management Review*, vol. 8, no. 3, pp. 377-387, DOI: 10.1080/14719030600853022.

Osborne S.P. (2010a), "The (New) Public Governance: a suitable case for treatment", Chap. 1 in *The New Public Governance?* London: Routledge.

Osborne S.P. (2010b), "Public governance and public service delivery: a research agenda for the future", Chap. 23 in *The New Public Governance?* London: Routledge.

Pires R.R.C. (2010), Flexibility, Consistency and Results in the Management of Bureaucratic Performance, *Working Paper IPEA/ILO/SIT*.

Pollitt C. (2009), Bureaucracies Remember, Post-Bureaucratic Organizations Forget?, *Public Administration*, vol. 87, no. 2, pp. 198-218, doi: 10.1111/J.1467-9299.2008.01738.X.

Pollitt, C., and Bouckaert, G. (2000), *Public management reform: An international comparison*, Oxford: Oxford University Press.

Powell W., White W., Koput D.R., Owen-Smith J., (2005), Network Dynamics and Field Evolution: The Growth of Interorganizational Collaboration in the Life Sciences, *American Journal Of Sociology*, vol. 110, n. 4, pp. 1132-1205. Doi: 10.1086/421508.

Power M., (1999), *The Audit Society*, Oxford: Oxford University Press.

Raadschelders J.C.N. (1995), Rediscovering Citizenship: Historical And Contemporary Reflections, *Public Administration*, vol. 73, no. 4, pp. 611-625. doi: 10.1111/j.1467-9299.1995.tb00849.x.

Rothstein, H., Downer, J. (2012), 'Renewing Defra': Exploring the emergence of risk-based policymaking in UK central government, *Public Administration*, vol. 90, pp. 781-799. doi:10.1111/j.1467-9299.2011.01999.x.

Seibel W. (2010), Beyond Bureaucracy – Public Administration as Political Integrator and Non-Weberian Thought in Germany, *Public Administration Review*, vol. 70, no. 5, pp. 719-730, doi: 10.1111/j.1540-6210.2010.02200.x.

Selznick, P. (1948), "Foundations of the theory of organizations", *American Sociological Review,* vol. 13, no. 1, pp. 25-35. doi: https://www.jstor.org/stable/2086752.

Shaw R., (2013), Another Size Fits all? Public Value Management and Challenges for Institutional Design, *Public Management Review*, Vol. 15, no. 4, pp. 477-500, doi: 10.1080/14719037.2012.664017.

Simon H. (1956), Rational choice and the structure of the environment, *Psychological Review*, vol. 63, no. 2, pp. 129-138. Doi: 10.1037/h0042769.

Sørensen E., and Torfing J., (2009), Making Governance Networks Effective And Democratic Through Metagovernance, *Public Administration*, Vol. 87, no. 2, pp. 234-258, DOI: 10.1111/j.1467-9299.2009.01753.x.

Tichelar, M. (1997), Professional bureaucracy as a barrier to management learning in the public services: A personal reflection, *Local Government Studies*, vol. 23, no. 2, pp. 14-25. doi: 10.1080/03003939708433862.

Vinot D. (2014), Transforming hospital management à la francaise: The new role of clinical managers in French public hospitals, *International Journal of Public Sector Management*, vol. 27 (5): 406-416, doi: 10.1108/IJPSM-06-2012-0067.

Voets J., Verhoest K., and Molenveld A. (2015), Coordinating for Integrated Youth Care: The need for smart metagovernance, *Public Management Review*, vol. 17, no. 7, pp. 981-1001, doi: 10.1080/14719037.2015.1029347.

Weber M., (1922), *Economy and Society*, Berkeley: University of California Press.

Weber M. (1946), *Essays in sociology*, New York: Oxford University Press.

Williams B.N., Kang S.-C., and Johnson J. (2016), (Co)-Contamination as the Dark Side of Co-Production: Public value failures in co-production processes, *Public Management Review*, vol. 18, no. 5, pp. 692-717, doi: 10.1080/14719037.2015.1111660.

Zafirovski M., (2001), Administration and Society: Beyond Public Choice? *Public Administration*, Vol. 79, no. 3, pp. 665-688, DOI: 10.1111/1467-9299.00274.

# Chapter 2

# DEVELOPING A BEHAVIORAL APPROACH IN PUBLIC ADMINISTRATIONS

SUMMARY: 1. Introduction. – 2. The behavioral approach in the private sector. – 3. The behavioral approach in the public sector. – 4. A proposed framework for studying the behavioral approach in the public sector. – 5. Locating the behavioral approach in the evolution of public administration. – 6. Final remarks. – 7. References.

## 1. Introduction

Starting from the gaps in the literature analyzed in the previous chapter, this chapter emphasizes the importance of individual behaviors in the public service environment as such behaviors shape, and are shaped by, personal qualities, interpersonal relationships, and context-related variables. The effects on dimensions such as leadership, human resource management, and interactions are also examined, relating these dimensions to both operational management and change management. If managers are willing to make good decisions and motivate their workforce, they need informed insight into the workings of their own minds and cognitions, in addition to a sense of humility about the degree of the complexity of their working environment.

This chapter aims to provide insights into the importance of individual behaviors, and to introduce a newer practical and theoretical approach to the analysis and interpretation of the issues mentioned above, addressing the inefficiencies and weaknesses related to the classic models of public administration (bureaucracy, NPM, and NPG).

The remainder of the chapter is structured as follows. The second section addresses the debate on the behavioral approach and its importance, building on the framework provided by Huse (2007) and on the literature grounded in the for-profit sector. The third section deepens the discussion of the issue of the behavioral approach in the public sector by also employing research on the ISI Web of Knowledge research engine. The fourth section, building on previous content, and moving on from the framework advanced by Huse (2007), builds an adapted theoretical framework, showing the main implications for the public sector. The fifth section explains how the behavioral approach should be collocated within studies on the public sector, highlighting its key features and the steps introduced with respect to the previous approaches and models of public administration. The last section presents final remarks and considerations.

## 2. The behavioral approach in the private sector

The literature grounded in the for-profit sector has devoted great attention to the behavioral approach. An interesting analysis of the behavioral approach is that of Huse (2007), although its focus is on board members' behaviors.

Huse (2007) delineated four dimensions to analyze organizations under a behavioral approach: board members, interactions, structures and leadership, and decision-making culture. The framework is shown in Figure 2.1.

**Figure 2.1.** Framework proposed by Huse (2007).

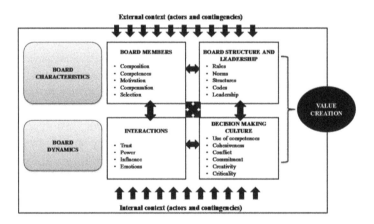

*Source:* own re-elaboration of the framework by Huse (2007).

The following subsections provide specific insights into each block of the framework, as analyzed by Hinna et al. (2014).

*Board members*

The first block includes four main concepts: board demography and composition, competences, motivation, and compensation.

*Board composition* is usually defined in terms of numbers of board members, the insider-outsider ratio, board tenure, and diversity (Finkelstein & Mooney, 2003; Milliken & Martins, 1996). These elements could positively or negatively influence the capability of board to carry out its tasks in various ways (Dalton et al., 1998; Forbes & Milliken, 1999; Horwitz & Horwitz, 2007; Lawrence, 1997; Melone, 1994). For example, resource dependence theorists argue that both board size and diversity contribute to superior board performance (Dalton et al., 1999; Jensen, 1993; Pfeffer & Salancik, 1978).

Within this area are also the *competences* of board members, referring to the presence of required knowledge, experiences, and skills: the background of each board member and their combination comprise a relevant element in performing the various tasks assigned to the board (Hillman & Dalziel, 2003; Johanisson & Huse, 2000; Nahapiet & Goshal, 1998).

Moreover, the board dynamics may benefit from *motivated individuals* (Steel & Konig, 2006): in corporate governance studies, professional standards, reputation, and awareness of liability have been labelled intrinsic motivation (Deci, 1975; Deci & Ryan, 1985). Other scholars argue that the main motivation for being board members is to represent those who elected them (Hermalin & Weisback, 1991; Huse, 2007). All these elements explain board behavior to a greater than the adopted mechanisms for *compensation* (Deci et al., 1998). However, compensation and incentives issues have also received considerable attention in the literature (Erez & Somech, 1996; Hermalin & Weisback, 1991; Kosnik, 1990). The most common thinking is that "high fixed compensation is an incentive to be a board member, while performance or activity based compensation serve as impetus for working on the board" (Huse, 2007, p. 78).

All these characteristics make possible the existence of a "market" of board members, for their election or *selection* (Huse, 2007).

## Interactions

According to Huse (2007), interactions are the more relevant issue in understanding the human side of corporate governance; indeed, they are probably the central core for explaining board dynamics. Pioneering studies on board behavior argue that interactional difficulties (i.e., process losses) prevent boards from achieving their full potential (Forbes & Milliken, 1999; Gibson & Earley, 2007). Coherent with the behavioral perspective, in this theoretical contribution the board is considered to be an open system with interactions between board members, the top management team, and various other actors, both inside and outside the boardroom (Pettigrew, 1992).

Different stakeholders exhibit significant differences in expectations. Furthermore, the divergence and convergence of stakeholders' expectations may provide an organization's management with critical leverage in using boards for stakeholder management (Huse & Eide, 1996).

Moving on to interactions inside the boardroom, the exchange of information is described and classified in terms of frequency of board meetings, frequency of interactions between the directors besides board meetings and frequency of face-to-face interactions between the directors, the main interaction partners. However, the roles played by boards also depend on the changing relationships between external and internal actors. Because of the pressures arising from the requests of the different actors involved, boards are liable to characterize issues differently and to hold different opinions about what the appropriate responses to these issues are (Dutton & Jackson, 1987).

In particular, board members have to interact with internal actors, especially the top management team, to shape strategic directions and to make informed decisions, protecting the interests of stakeholders (Hendry & Kiel, 2004; Huse, 2007; McNulty & Pettigrew, 1999; Stiles & Taylor, 2001).

*Power* is another important issue in board dynamics (Mintzberg, 1983; Pearce & Zahra, 1991; Pettigrew & McNulty, 1995): through the exercise of power, board members may contribute (more or less) to strategizing in the boardroom (Bunderson & Sutcliffe, 2003; Johnson et al., 2003; Ravasi & Zattoni, 2006; Zajac & Westphal, 1996). According to Dahl (1957), "*An individual has power over another individual to the extent that the former can get the latter to do something that the latter would not otherwise do*" (p. 202). In addition, power as a relation between actors is linked to the concept of *influence* (Huse, 2007; Pettigrew & McNulty, 1998; Yukl, 1998). The literature (Finkelstein, 1992; Huse & Eide, 1996; Luhman, 1988; Lukes, 1974) defines different types of power (direct, indirect …), but with particular reference to board dynamics it is important to stress that power and influence could both induce the creation of alliances inside and outside the boardroom and also explain the political dynamics (Michels, 1962; Ocasio, 1994).

To understand relationships among actors, and behaviors more generally, the role of *trust* is also an essential element (Bromiley & Cummings, 1995; Browing et al., 1995; McAllister, 1995; Huse, 2007, 1998; Hosmer, 1995, Korsgaard et al., 1995; Larson, 1992). Some scholars (Donaldson, 1990; Donaldson & Davis, 1991; Huse, 1990, 2000) have defined trust as an important "bidirectional" control mechanism, used both by principal and agent. Most studies of boards and governance make implicit assumptions about trust, but few studies are precise in defining the term; consequently, it is possible to distinguish, for example, between competence-based trust and integrity-based types of trust (Hosmer, 1995; Ring, 1996;

Sapienza et al., 2000). In this area, Huse also refers to *emotions*: these could be manifested with different degrees of intensity during working processes; they may reflect rationality or irrationality; they evolve during time; they may restrain or drive behaviors (Brundin, 2002; Brundin & Nordqvist, 2008).

## Structures and leadership

The third block, structures and leadership, refers to all the elements that constrain, empower, or facilitate actions and behaviors within the boardroom. First, the presence, or the creation, of formal and informal *rules and norms* may moderate the dynamics among board members (Ocasio, 1999; Patton & Baker, 1987; Westphal & Zajac, 1998). Also, the various national codes of good governance provide some recommendations regarding behaviors of actors working within the boardroom (Higgs, 2003; Monks & Minow, 2004; Roberts et al., 2005). Norms, rules, and codes could reflect both the needs and requests of internal and external actors (Westphal & Zajac, 1998). According to Jonnergard and Stafsuddthe (2011), an interplay of cognitive and political factors is fundamental in not only generating but also maintaining the rules and routines that structure behavior.

*Board structures and leadership* also contribute to explaining this block (Finkelstein et al., 2008). The concept of leadership (Roberts et al., 2005) refers to the roles, attributes, and styles of the board chair: CEO duality, in fact, is one of the most studied issues in relation to board structures and leadership (Dalton et al., 1998). Moreover, board structure is defined by the establishment of committees (audit, control, nomination, remuneration, etc.), and board instructions (working documents that describe the activities of the board and how the board is to meet its tasks) (Osterloh & Frey, 2004).

## Decision-making culture

The last area of interest in studying board dynamics concerns the decision-making culture, characterizing the board as a team (Forbes & Milliken, 1999; Leblanc & Gillies, 2005; Smith et al., 1994; Stiles & Taylor, 2001). The decision-making culture is defined, *inter alia*, using several concepts, such as cognitive conflict, cohesiveness, commitment, creativity, and criticality.

The definitions of tasks elements, such as strategy or policy development and implementation, access both the affective reactions of decision makers and cognitive processing (Amason, 1996; Dutton & Jackson, 1987; Gibson & Earley, 2007; Huber & Lewis, 2010). Decision-making processes involve not only board members, but also internal and external actors, in relations that could be characterized by several kinds of *conflict*. First, cognitive conflict refers to judgmental differences about how best to achieve organizational objectives; it is based on technical disagreements regarding how information might be interpreted (Amason, 1996; Berg, 2007; Higashide & Birley, 2002). In addition, both personal incompatibilities and different preferences or values (Amason, 1996) determine the development of affective conflict, which tends to be emotional and more ideological in nature. Here, there may not be a political consensus among actors over the weight assigned to particular outcomes, especially outcomes involving non-monetary impacts (Berg, 2007, p. 4).

Therefore, defining board tasks, and interpretation of political, and social issues activates and motivates the protection of power and resources by board members (Narayanan & Fahey, 1982), predicting both cognitive and affective conflicts (Burns, 1962; Daft & Weick, 1984; Jehn, 1997; Thomas et al., 1994).

An important element in the resolution (or not) of conflicts could be the way in which board members use their knowledge and skills: if they are willing to give advice based on their knowledge, to share in an open and generous manner ideas, suggestions, and points of view, the performance and the effectiveness of boards will probably increase (Cadbury, 2002; Melone, 1994; Shropshire, 2010; Sonnenfeld, 2002). This construct refers to the board's ability to tap into the knowledge and skills available to it, and then to apply them to its tasks. It also represents the occurrence of collective learning among members (Hackman, 1987). However, the use of knowledge and skills is different from cognitive conflict: the former refers to the process by which members' contributions are coordinated, the latter refers to the content of members' contributions.

However, other dimensions also describe the board's decision-making culture. *Commitment* can be defined as the board members' expectations concerning the intensity of individual behavior (Forbes & Milliken, 1999; Huse, 2007). Board *cohesiveness* refers to the degree to which board members are attracted to each other and are motivated to remain on the board (Forbes & Millken, 1999; Huse & Soldberg, 2006). It is also expressed by a good atmosphere during work meetings; indeed, cohesiveness captures the affective dimension of members' inclusion on the board and reflects the ability of the board to continue working together (Summers et al., 1988). *Creativity* is the ability to find creative solutions to problems or to innovate in working practices in the boardroom (Huse, 2007). Finally, *criticality* is about the real independence of each board member in behavior, and consequently in decision-making processes (Huse, 2007).

## 3. The behavioral approach in the public sector

The previous section, building on the framework provided by Huse (2007) and on the literature grounded in the for-profit sector, has shown that many studies have discussed the behavioral approach in the private sector.

While in the literature grounded in the for-profit sector there is a stream of research on behavioral dimensions exploring "*actors, decisions making processes, relationships and interactions inside and outside the boardroom*" (Gabrielsson & Huse, 2004, p. 19), the public sector literature presents few studies examining behavioral issues (Hinna, et al., 2010).

As Skelcher (1998) pointed out, it is expedient to carry out an in-depth analysis of public organizations' internal and external functioning, while few years later Cornforth (2003) asked for a deeper understanding of competencies, skills, abilities, and behaviors of public organizations, as could be found in the literature on corporate governance (Forbes & Milliken, 1999).

The literature on the public sector has mainly concentrated on aspects related to governance, with a specific focus on the analysis of expectations concerning boards' tasks in public administrations, providing evidence related to strategic tasks (Dopson et al., 1999; Jørgensen, 1999; Sullivan et al., 2006), control tasks (Clatworthy et al., 2000; Considine, 2000; Hood et al., 2000; Hyndman & Eden, 2001; Midttun & Kamfjord, 1999; Sanderson, 2002; Siciliano, 2002; Smith & Beazley, 2000; West & Durant, 2000), or networking tasks (Klijn & Skelcher, 2007; Lowndes & Wilson, 2003).

Few scholars have investigated human aspects, although some have considered boards of directors (Benz & Frey, 2007; Boyne & Dahya, 2002; Conforth & Edwards, 1999; Greer & Hoggett, 2000; Kirkbride & Letza, 2003). Indeed, as recently pointed out by Cornforth (2012), even if the governing body has the main responsibility for carrying out governance functions, the organizational system is wider than this, and includes the framework of responsibilities, requirements, and accountabilities within which public (and non-profit) organizations operate. Moreover, it also includes other actors within organizations, such as managers, members, and other groups that may contribute to carrying out governance and management functions.

This opens up the scope of research examining the behavioral implications for public organizations in managing the system of relationships, focusing on the relationship between internal and "external" actors (stakeholders), and the relationship between the management and other public employees (Gnan et al., 2013).

The results of the literature review conducted in the first chapter show that only three papers discuss the behavioral approach. Thus, in this chapter more specific research has been conducted to verify how many papers effectively concern individual behaviors in the public sector, and in what terms. This research employed the keywords "*behavior AND public administration*" to search the ISI Web of Knowledge research engine. A further selection was made according to the following criteria: document type "article," language "English," research area "public administration," topic "individual." This selection resulted in the identification of 41 papers. Of these, 14 papers were found not to be coherent with the aim of this research, while 4 papers focused on existing bias in the methods used to analyze behaviors in the public sector domain, and one paper focused on the need to study public employees' behaviors through a psychological lens.

The remaining 22 papers were labeled as in Table 2.1.

**Table 2.1.** Studies emerging from the research.

| Label | N |
|---|---|
| Behaviors related to issues concerning HRM (such as selection, motivation, competences, incentives, personality, gender) | 9 |
| Behaviors related to issues concerning organizational structure and culture (such as rules and norms, culture and values, structures and task characteristics, leadership, ethics, and integrity) | 7 |
| Behaviors related to issues concerning interactions (such as trust, power, emotions, influence) | 3 |
| Behaviors related to issues concerning organizational climate (such as conflict, commitment, job context) | 3 |

As can clearly be seen from the table, a major focus has been devoted to aspects concerning the "hard" part of the organization, such as human resource management and structure, culture, and values, while less attention is paid to "soft" aspects, such as individual interactions and organizational climate.

Papers that can be ascribed within the first category contend that employees' behaviors are affected by personal motivation (Chen & Hsieh, 2015; De Simone et al., 2016; Harari et al., 2017; Homberg et al., 2015; Piatak, 2015, 2016; Van Witteloostuijn et al., 2017), core personality traits (Van Witteloostuijn et al., 2017), and gender (Nielsen, 2015). Public service motivation (PSM), in fact, has been found to influence job satisfaction and engagement (De Simone et al., 2016; Homberg et al., 2015); it has also been found to influence civil servants' interest in policy making and commitment to the public interest (Chen & Hsieh, 2015), thus influencing in turn their behaviors. Nielsen (2015) has found that street-level bureaucrats' behaviors vary depending on personal characteristics such as gender, even if the effects of these behaviors are conditioned by the regulatory institutions of the specific task to be carried out. Van Witteloostuijn et al. (2017) find that PSM is strongly influenced by core personality traits. In particular, affective motives of PSM – compassion and self-sacrifice – are positively influenced by the personality traits of honesty-humility, emotionality, and agreeableness, and negatively by conscientiousness. In contrast, non-affective PSM motives – attraction to policy making and commitment to the public interest – are positively associated with the openness to experience trait.

Papers that can be ascribed within the second category contend that employees' behaviors are affected by aspects related to organizational structure and culture, such as rules and norms (Cabral & Lazzarini, 2015), culture and values (Wright, 2015; Wynen & Verhoest, 2015), structures and task characteristics (Anton et al., 2014; Tummers et al., 2015), ethical leadership, ethics and integrity (Kolthoff, 2016; Svara, 2014). Authors highlighting the role of rules and norms (Cabral & Lazzarini, 2015) raise the issue of the need to "guard the guardians," that is, the problem of monitoring public officials' behaviors when judging their peers. Cabral and Lazzarini (2015) highlight that in certain situations, public officials often turn a blind eye, thus refraining from punishing their peers.

Culture and values are linked by Wright (2015) to behaviors, as the author refers to Dahl's (1957) assumptions that public administration is plagued by three interrelated problems (culture, values, and behaviors). The reason for this assumption is that it has always been argued that public administration could establish a set of principles that would have universal validity, independent of moral or political ends, individual human differences, or social influences. This concept seems to be related strictly to the presumption of perfect rationality and to the lack of recognition of a bounded rationality (Simon, 1956), which has driven (and still drives) politicians and bureaucrats.

Structures and task characteristics have been found to determine public employees' efforts and behavioral intentions, as task characteristics that lead to work alienation result in less effort and greater intention to leave (Tummers et al., 2015), while the perceived usefulness of structures and technologies among employees influences their behavioral intentions (Anton et al., 2014).

Authors addressing the key role of ethics and integrity, and the need to develop ethical leadership (Kolthoff, 2016; Svara, 2014), highlight that a code of ethics is required within public organizations, as is a broadening of the awareness of the ethical responsibilities of all public administrators among society (Svara, 2014). Based on the same precept, Kolthoff (2016) contends that ethics and integrity are fundamental instruments against white collar unethical behaviors, and to prevent and control organizational crime and human rights violations.

Papers that can be ascribed within the third category contend that employees' behaviors are affected by aspects related to individual interactions, such as trust and emotions (Chen et al., 2014; Ko & Hur, 2014), and power and influence (Vandenabeele et al., 2014). Workplace trust and behaviors are the result of human interaction and personal choices, which in turn have a bearing on individual motivation (Chen et al., 2014). Again, trust and procedural justice have an impact on the relationships between employee benefits and work attitudes (Ko & Hur, 2014). Also, power and influence are found to affect individual behaviors: Vandenabeele et al. (2014) highlight the role of transformational leadership in promoting public values and in developing PSM; in particular, the authors found that a positive relation between leadership and PSM exists and that it is moderated by a set of basic psychological needs (autonomy and competence).

Papers that can be ascribed within the last category contend that employees' behaviors are affected by aspects related to organizational climate, such as conflict, commitment, and job context. Oldenhof et al. (2014) highlight the role of compromise in solving conflict. In particular, the authors assert that managers have to perform continuous "justification work" that entails not only the use of rhetoric, but also the adaptation of behaviors and material objects; by this means, managers are able to solidify compromises, thereby creating temporary stability in times of organizational change.

Kim et al. (2015) argue that increased responsibility and commitment are central to understanding individual and collective behaviors and performance. The authors contend that increased commitment leads to higher levels of PSM, and thus employees are much more motivated to engage in prosocial behaviors that benefit others. Due to the impact of commitment on PSM and on employees' behaviors, Kim et al. (2015) suggest attention to job characteristics and the dynamic nature of PSM is important in particularly stressful front-line professions.

Finally, stressing the importance of the job context, Campbell (2017) highlights how job context characteristics, and especially hierarchical position, shape the effects of transformational leadership on employee rule perception and on their consequent behavior. In greater detail, the problem of organizational red tape is emphasized, defined as "*rules, regulations, and procedures that remain in force and entail a compliance burden, but do not advance the legitimate purposes the rules were intended to serve*" (Bozeman, 2000, p. 12), the perception of which may be influenced by transformational leadership. Thus, according to Campbell (2017), a better understanding of how the organizational context shapes employees' perceptions of rules can help leaders promote positive work attitudes and performance.

## 4. A proposed framework for studying the behavioral approach in the public sector

It is worth noting that Huse (2007), not only refers to the private sector, but predominantly the board of directors; thus, additional effort is made in this section to adapt the framework to the whole organization, rather than narrowly focusing on directors.

As shown in the previous section, several interesting aspects can be considered in analyzing behaviors within the public sector. Starting from the results emerging from the aforementioned research, a tentative approach may be made in building a framework that integrates the aspects highlighted. Thus, the proposed framework brings together hard and soft aspects of organization, delineating four main blocks, two for each aspect. In greater detail, hard aspects may be recognized as those related to human resource management and to the characteristics concerning organizational structure and culture (also including managerial/leadership styles). Soft aspects may be recognized as those concerning individual and organizational dynamics, such as interactions and features influencing the organizational climate.

Figure 2.2 shows Huse's framework adapted to incorporate the aforementioned aspects with a view to being useful in comprehending and analyzing behavioral factors within public organizations.

**Figure 2.2.** Proposed framework for the adoption of the behavioral approach in public organizations.

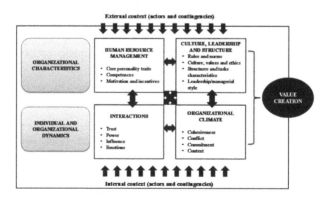

*Source:* own adaptation of the framework by Huse (2007) to the public sector.

The following subsections provide specific descriptions for each block of the framework.

## Human resource management

The first block includes the main concepts related to human resource management: core personality traits, competences, motivation, and incentives. Personal characteristics and traits have been found to influence individual behaviors (Nielsen, 2015; Van Witteloostuijn et al., 2017); thus, in selecting employees there is the need to verify, initially and periodically, the alignment of their personalities with organizational targets and values. Examples of sensitive issues concerning employees' selection are traits such as gender, and characteristics such as honesty, humility, emotionality, agreeableness, and openness (Van Witteloostuijn et al., 2017). These characteristics are influenced by the specific tasks to be carried out, but they may simultaneously influence the way in which tasks are carried out.

The *competences* of members refer to the presence of the *knowledge, experiences,* and *skills* required: the background of each individual and their combination are relevant to optimal performance of the tasks assigned (Hillman & Dalziel, 2003; Johanisson & Huse, 2000; Nahapiet & Goshal, 1998). This is key in consideration of the particular attention that has to be paid to the correspondence between job position and personal characteristics and competences.

Clearly, the organization may benefit from *motivated individuals* (Steel & Konig, 2006): within this category are both intrinsic and extrinsic motivation, considering all approaches related to the needs and aspirations that drive individuals' motivation (Alderfer, 1969; Lock & Latham, 1990; Maslow, 1954; McClelland, 1961). The theme of motivation in the public sector is particularly sensitive and has prompted an intense stream of research (e.g., Crewson, 1997; Houston, 2000; Moynihan & Pandey, 2007; Perry, 1996, 1997). This is especially due to low motivation and other negative effects, often associated with the standardized tasks to be carried out within bureaucracies.

However, *incentives and compensation* issues have also received considerable attention in literature (Erez & Somech, 1996; Hermalin & Weisback, 1991; Kosnik, 1990). According to Huse (2007), the most common thinking is that while high fixed compensation is an incentive, performance- or activity-based compensation serves as a greater impetus for working. This is the key aspect upon which the new public management (NPM) approach relies, namely by providing "rewards" for individual performance. The concept is primarily related to the aforementioned problem of low motivation associated with repetitive tasks; thus, to avoid alienation and turnover, the general idea is to increase incentives related to – sometimes easily reached – specific goals.

On the basis of these elements, a *selection* process that finds the right balance should be carried out. This process may clearly encounter difficulties in those countries where selection is related to a system based on public bids. This obviously guarantees the respect of criteria such as transparency and meritocracy, but at the same time it represents a limit on the managerial actions of selection, evaluation, and promotion, leading to reduced possibilities for managers to choose employees and resources freely for their teams.

## Culture, leadership, and structures

The second block, "culture, leadership, and structures," refers to all the elements making up the organizational structure and superstructure that may influence individual behaviors, such as rules and norms, culture and values, ethics and integrity, structure and task characteristics, leadership and managerial styles.

The presence or the creation of formal and informal *rules and norms* may regulate, moderate, and influence individual dynamics (Ocasio, 1999; Patton & Baker, 1987; Westphal & Zajac, 1998). This is particularly true of public organizations, in which the bureaucratic imprinting on the tasks to be carried out strongly influences the way in which employees work and interact by engendering situations such as alienation and turnover.

Norms, rules, and codes could reflect both the needs and the requirements of internal and external actors (Westphal & Zajac, 1998). While norms and rules may predominantly regulate life within organization, codes (such as those of ethics or those establishing organizational values and culture formally or informally) regulate not only the way in which individuals behave within the organization, but also their behaviors as representatives of the organization in the external context. This, of course, should be especially true for public sector organizations as these are *multi-stakeholder* structures with a main objective to manage and gain legitimacy through public consensus (Gnan et al., 2013). In this regard, culture and values, as well as ethics and integrity, are fundamental instruments against white collar unethical behaviors, and preventing and controlling organizational crime and human rights violations (Kolthoff, 2016). Establishing a code of ethics within public organizations thus becomes a prominent means of broadening awareness of the ethical responsibilities and accountability of public administrators in terms of the public interest (Svara, 2014).

Also, structures, task characteristics, and leadership/managerial styles contribute to explaining the block "Culture, leadership, and structures" of the framework (Finkelstein et al., 2008). In particular, the idea of leadership (Roberts et al., 2005) refers to the roles, attributes, and styles of managers (Dalton et al., 1998). The way in which managers behave influences the way in which employees behave: unethical behaviors, unfair leadership/managerial attitudes, and lack of accountability have a similar effect on different forms of integrity violations, including corruption and human rights violations (Huberts et al., 2007; Kolthoff, 2016).

Structures and task characteristics are key in determining public employees' effort and behavioral intentions, since task characteristics that lead to work alienation result in less effort and greater intention to leave (Tummers et al., 2015), while employees' perceptions of the usefulness of structures and technologies influences their behavioral intentions, their work performance, and the quality of the tasks they have to carry out (Anton et al., 2014).

## Interactions

Interactions are among the most relevant issues in understanding the human side of organizations and explaining individual dynamics. Studies of individual behaviors argue that interactional difficulties often affect individual work performance and threaten the achievement of the full potential in the task to be performed (Forbes & Milliken, 1999; Gibson & Earley, 2007).

As public organizations are made up of a multitude of actors and encompass the interests of multiple stakeholders, in this discussion we consider them to be open systems characterized by interactions among these actors (board members, managers, officers, employees, the community, and other public stakeholders) participating in different ways in the life of the public organizations (Pettigrew, 1992). In this context, behaviors are affected by aspects related to individual interactions, such as trust and emotions (Chen et al., 2014; Ko & Hur, 2014), power and influence (Vandenabeele et al., 2014). The role of trust is an essential element in understanding relationships among actors and behaviors more generally (Bromiley & Cummings, 1995; Browning et al., 1995; Huse, 2007, 1998; Hosmer, 1995, Korsgaard et al., 1995; Larson, 1992; McAllister, 1995). Workplace trust is at the base of individual interactions: the lower the trust between two individuals, the lower the level of interaction between them. The same can be shown in the case of emotions as they may be considered the engine that boosts positive or negative reactions to counterparts' behaviors. In addition, emotions can be manifested with different degrees of intensity during work processes; they may reflect rationality or irrationality, they evolve during time, and they may constrain or drive behaviors (Brundin, 2002; Brundin & Nordqvist, 2008).

Power and influence are also important issues in individual dynamics (Mintzberg, 1983; Pearce & Zahra, 1991; Pettigrew & McNulty, 1995). Indeed, power as a relation between actors is strongly linked to the concept of influence (Huse, 2007; Pettigrew & McNulty, 1998; Yukl, 1998). These variables also explain the political dynamics within organizations, leading to the creation of alliances or contrapositions among different groups or individuals (Michels, 1962; Ocasio, 1994).

Through the exercise of power and influence over others, individuals can assure the achievement of their goals. Such power and influence can be exerted in both direct and indirect ways, sometimes assuming the features of suggestions, especially when an informal relationship exists between two people. In this way, it is possible to influence people to do things, thus not necessarily having recourse to a coercive approach. Power and influence are thus at the core of individuals' relationships; they are also a fundamental part of individuals' needs to be achieved to increase personal motivation (McClelland, 1961). On this basis, power and influence strongly affect individual behaviors: Vandenabeele et al. (2014) highlight the role of transformational leadership in promoting public values and in developing PSM; in particular, the authors find that there is a positive relation between leadership and PSM, and that it is moderated by a set of basic psychological needs (autonomy and competence).

## Organizational climate

The last area of interest in studying individual behaviors is related to the organizational climate. Organizational climate is greatly affected by several variables concerning the way in which individuals behave and interact with others, such as the degree of conflict, the degree of individual commitment, the degree of cohesiveness, and other contextual factors.

The degree of conflict characterizing a specific context, might influence not only the way in which employees carry out their activities, but also the informal relationship with others (Amason, 1996; Dutton & Jackson, 1987; Gibson & Earley, 2007; Huber & Lewis, 2010). This in turn might create a loop that leads to an increasing level of conflict, negatively affecting overall organizational performance.

As previously highlighted, conflict may be cognitive and affective with regard to the different situations that lead to its emergence. A *cognitive conflict*, based on technical disagreements, refers to judgmental differences about how best to achieve organizational objectives, and might emerge when the same information is interpreted in different ways by different individuals.

*Affective conflict* is related to both personal incompatibilities and different preferences or values, and tends to be emotional and more ideological in nature.

Both cognitive and affective conflicts are important topics of investigation with regard to the public governance debate (Hinna & Scarozza, 2015; Tomo et al., 2016), as public administrations face specific challenges related to multiple, conflicting, and ambiguous goals.

Therefore, in defining tasks, political and social issues should be considered, especially in terms of possible consequences due to interpretation, and the protection of power and resources that might activate employees' reactions (Narayanan & Fahey, 1982), by this means trying to predict both cognitive and affective conflicts (Burns, 1962; Daft & Weick, 1984; Jehn, 1997; Thomas et al., 1994).

An important element in the resolution (or not) of conflicts could be the development of *negotiation skills*, especially for public managers. This point is key in establishing instruments useful for reducing the level of conflict, or avoiding its emergence. In this regard, the study by Kahnemann (2011) on how people reason and react to specific situations might be of great support. This could also help in understanding the right way in which individuals may *use their knowledge and skills* to share in an open and generous way ideas, suggestions, and points of view (Cadbury, 2002; Melone, 1994; Shropshire, 2010; Sonnenfeld, 2002).

Reducing or avoiding conflict positively influences the level of *commitment* and *cohesiveness*, and supports a good atmosphere in the work context, capturing the affective dimension of members' inclusion and increasing the ability and the willingness of people to continue working together (Summers et al., 1988).

## 5. Locating the behavioral approach in the evolution of public administration

This section aims to clarify how the behavioral approach might be located within the studies on public sector administration. With this aim in mind, the study by Geddes (2012) provides an interesting review of the previous models of public administration: public administration (PA) (Taylor, 1947; Weber, 1922, cited in Gerth and Mills, 1948); new public management (NPM) (Hood, 1991; Osborne & Gaebler, 1992); collaborative public management (CPM) (Agranoff & McGuire, 2003; Kickert et al., 1997).

Geddes (2012, p. 951) provides a table that summarizes the different public administration models, based on 11 management dimensions: performance, accountability, community engagement, values, leadership, employment relations, management tasks, decision making, structure, processes, and change. The author, through her study, delineates the prevailing management model for each dimension (Geddes, 2012, p. 953). Geddes' Table 2 is adapted here to highlight the potential contribution of the behavioral approach to the picture of public administration studies.

While one could agree or not with the results emerging from Geddes' research, here the aim is to provide possible solutions based on the behavioral approach applied to previous models' inefficiencies.

**Table 2.2.** Solutions proposed by the behavioral approach.

| Management dimension | Prevailing management model | Key aspects of the model | Behavioral approach | Authors |
|---|---|---|---|---|
| Performance | CPM | Network; outcomes; cross-cutting and renegotiable objectives | Improve relationships and individual behaviors | Campbell (2017); Chen et al. (2014); Ko and Hur (2014) |
| Accountability | NPM | To contracts; individual/manager | Improve individual accountability towards the community and all public stakeholders | Kim et al. (2015) |
| Community engagement | PA | Client; minimum public information and engagement; one-size fits all | Improve community engagement in the decision-making process | Agranoff and McGuire (2003); Kickert et al. (1997) |
| Values | PA | Public service ethics; probity; impartiality; consistency; equity; risk minimization | Improve mutuality, reciprocity, and ethics in the public interest, not only in the public service | Cabral and Lazzarini (2015); Wright (2015); Wynen and Verhoest (2015) |
| Leadership | CPM | Natural; facilitative; participative | Develop transformational, merit appointed, facilitative, participative, but also ethical and accountable leadership | Campbell (2017); Kolthoff (2016); Svara (2014); Vandenabeele et al. (2014) |

*see next page*

| | | | | |
|---|---|---|---|---|
| Employment relations | PA | Personnel management; national pay rates; stable careers; role specialization; manager appraisal; staff training | Improve employees' motivation with monetary incentives, non-monetary incentives, increasing commitment and participation, reducing repetitive tasks, and increasing employees' responsibility | Chen and Hsieh (2015); Nielsen (2015); Homberg et al. (2015) |
| Management tasks | CPM | Network/process manager: activation; framing; mobilizing; synthesizing | Improve managers' skills in negotiation, and in ethical and cultural management | Kolthoff (2016); Svara (2014) |
| Decision making | CPM | Evidence based; joint stakeholders; integrated policy implementation and evaluation | Improve adaptive management | Artinger et al. (2014); Bauer et al. (2013) |
| Structure | CPM | Network; pluralistic; multiple agencies; inter-agency; permeable supported boundaries | Maintain hierarchy, but develop responsibility; increase flexibility | Anton et al. (2014); Campbell (2017); Tummers et al. (2015) |
| Processes | CPM | Covenants/compacts; commissioning; pooled budget; integrated technology | Reduce formalism; introduce management by projects to increase flexibility and individual responsibility | Kim et al. (2015) |
| Change | CPM | Experimental; bottom-up; continuous improvement | Both cultural and structural, but shared and oriented to improvement | Cabral and Lazzarini (2015); Wright (2015); Wynen and Verhoest (2015) |

*Source:* own elaboration based on Geddes, 2012, p. 953.
*Notes:* CPM denotes collaborative public management; NPM denotes new public management; PA denotes public administration.

Table 2.2 provides interesting insights into the behavioral approach that deserve in-depth discussion. Geddes (2012) asserts that in looking at *performance*, the prevailing model is collaborative public management (CPM). This model is based on considering the network as an entity to be accountable to in terms of outcomes, and based on cross-cutting and renegotiable objectives. While this might be an interesting and prominent aspect under a collaborative approach toward the improvement of external relationships, it does not focus on the aspects internal to the public administration. The reference here is to the need to improve relationships and individual behaviors within the public administration (Campbell, 2017; Chen et al., 2014; Ko & Hur, 2014) as negative relationships and behaviors may have an impact on both the organizational climate and performance, thus negatively affecting how the administration is perceived by external (public) stakeholders.

In terms of *accountability*, Geddes (2012) categorized NPM as the prevailing model. NPM assigns individual accountability to contracts, considering public managers and employees as "contractualized" individuals who should be accountable for what is stated in their contracts. On the one hand, this should ensure that individuals accomplish their tasks according to pre-defined conditions, thus "forecasting" all possible situations that might occur. On the other hand, this might not be sufficient considering bounded rationality (Simon, 1956), which characterizes the human mind and the theory of incomplete contracts (Grossman & Hart, 1986), according to which it is impossible to consider all the possible choices to be undertaken both by the human mind and by contracts. Thus, the behavioral approach shares the view of recognizing individual accountability, but this might be considered in relation to the community and all public stakeholders (Kim et al., 2015).

Considering *community engagement*, Geddes (2012) suggests public administration (PA) as the prevailing model, based on minimum public information and engagement, and on the concept of "one-size fits all." Clearly, this model refers to the community as a passive actor, and it is much more oriented to a sort of "mass production," according to which citizens are a unique and indistinct mass. While this concept might be shared in a "local" world, as it was in the first 50 or 60 years of the 20th century, today the globalization process also requires a structural change within public administration, including increased community engagement in the decision-making process. Thus, the behavioral approach shares the view of CPM (Agranoff & McGuire, 2003; Kickert et al., 1997), which considers citizens to be an active part within the public service provision process, defining choice, quality, and responsiveness related to the public service.

In terms of *values*, Geddes (2012) again identifies the PA model as prevalent. The PA model is built on values such as public service ethics, probity, impartiality, consistency, equity, and risk minimization. This because the PA model considers limiting public employees' responsibilities only to those aspects provided by their contracts. On the one hand, this has engendered situations in which public employees do not take risks that are far from what is stated in their contracts; on the other hand, this has led to phenomena such as the "displacement of goals" (Merton, 1940) and "work to rule" (Blau, 1955). Indeed, the behavioral approach intends to promote values such as mutuality, reciprocity, and ethics, oriented not only to public service, but also to the *public interest* (Cabral & Lazzarini, 2015; Wright, 2015; Wynen & Verhoest, 2015).

The prevailing model considering *leadership*, has been set out by Geddes (2012), i.e., CPM, which attributes to leadership characteristics such as natural, facilitative, and participative.

Improvement in this kind of leadership should consider the fact that to be recognized by the group, a leader requires not only transformational abilities, but also competences in terms of work tasks. Thus, the goal to be attained in terms of leadership, is to develop it around characteristics, such as merit appointed, transformational, facilitative, participative, but also ethical and accountable (Campbell, 2017; Kolthoff, 2016; Svara, 2014; Vandenabeele et al., 2014).

*Employment relations* represents one of the most sensitive aspects within public administration. Again, Geddes (2012) delineated PA as the prevailing model, namely one that is based on high specialization, stable careers, staff training, manager appraisal, and national pay rates. This model has repeatedly been indicated as leading to alienation and turnover (Mintzberg, 1979) due to the excessive standardization related to the tasks to be carried out by public servants, thus also lowering their motivation and negatively affecting their behaviors. The solution proposed is to improve employees' motivation, not only through monetary incentives introduced by NPM, but also by finding other non-monetary solutions, such as increasing commitment and participation, and reducing repetitive tasks (Chen & Hsieh, 2015; Homberg et al., 2015; Nielsen, 2015). This is necessary, but not sufficient if not accompanied by increased individual responsibility related to low performance or missed goals.

The prevailing model with regard to the *management task* dimension is CPM. Geddes (2012) highlights that "*Adroit managers activate and mobilize other managers to build and shape the nexus, developing capacity through searching for and assembling the right resources to enhance service delivery*" (p. 959). Thus, according to Geddes (2012), public managers' tasks should mainly be oriented toward networking and activating partnerships, thus mobilizing resources and improving the reputation of their public administration. Here the reference appears once again to be focused greatly on the external context, leaving unresolved several issues concerning the internal context of the public organization. For instance, one prominent aspect highlighted above in Section 4 is conflict management and the problem of cohesiveness. It has been argued that a lower level of conflict and a high degree of cohesiveness within the organization may help in attaining better performances, both in terms of quality of service and improved relationships within the PA. Thus, a critical skill to be developed, and continuously trained, is the negotiating ability of a public manager. Clearly, this should be accompanied by the ability to develop ethical and cultural management (Kolthoff, 2016; Svara, 2014).

Considering *decision-making*, the prevailing model set out by Geddes (2012) is CPM. Within this model, the author asserts that *"decisions are based on a joint assessment of each service user's needs and risks, stimulating alternatives that otherwise may not be considered, producing synergies as well as being a mechanism to keep all partners on board. This evidence base for action acts as an insurance policy against human error. Decision-making is incremental, proceeded by adjustment, convergence and closure, characterized by successive marginal adjustments due to the inability to accurately predict service user behaviour despite a range of structured assessment tools designed for that purpose"* (Geddes, 2012, p. 960).

While it is interesting that decision-making should be incremental and proceed by adjustments, and although it is argued that it is impossible to predict service user behavior, there is no reference to the fact that managers should reason concerning the possible outcomes that may derive from a certain action taken, especially considering that they are taking decisions in the public interest. Thus, here the possible solution is to adopt adaptive management (Artinger et al., 2014; Bauer et al., 2013), varying the managerial style relative to the understanding of the specific situation.

Geddes (2012) argues for CPM as the prevailing model considering *structure*. CPM considers as its main structure the network, based on multiple actors, agencies, and inter-relations. The boundaries of the organization are permeable and vary in consideration of the external actors included – or not – in different situations. While this represents an improved step towards openness to the external context with respect to the bureaucratic model, the literature has also argued that as post-bureaucratic models are much more flexible and open, with fewer rules, there is the risk of losing control over activities and engendering opportunistic behaviors. Thus, here the possible solution might be to consider maintaining hierarchy and rules, but also increasing responsibility and flexibility (Anton et al., 2014; Campbell, 2017; Tummers et al., 2015).

Linked strongly to the structural aspect, there is the dimension related to *processes*. Even in this case, the prevailing model is CPM, which as it considers the network as a structure also views processes as the result of covenants and commissioning, with a pooled budget and integrated technology. Here, despite the interesting openness to partnerships and shared processes, the focus is again outside the public administration. Before finding solutions outside, it is important to imagine how to solve internal issues to avoid low quality in public service and low organizational performance. A solution that might present a move toward this aim could be to reduce formalism and introduce management by projects. This would increase flexibility and individual responsibility (Kim et al., 2015), thus also affecting positively other management dimensions, such as employee relations, structure, performance, values, and accountability.

Finally, considering *change*, the prevalent model is CPM. CPM sees change as an experimental and bottom-up process, based on continuous improvement. While there is a shared the view of the need to improve continuously, here it is argued that change must be a shared process, neither necessarily top-down nor bottom-up, which might be of interest in terms of both cultural and structural aspects (Cabral & Lazzarini, 2015; Wright, 2015; Wynen & Verhoest, 2015), thus having a wider impact on the organization.

## 6. Final remarks

This chapter has discussed the main features of the behavioral approach. This has been undertaken by first assessing the literature in the for-profit sector, also drawing upon the framework provided by Huse (2007), which has prompted several studies on the behavioral approach and its importance.

It has been argued that research in the for-profit sector has devoted great attention to the behavioral approach, even if the accent has mainly been put on the board of directors. In this regard, the framework provided by Huse (2007) also analyzed behaviors within the board of directors through four main dimensions: "*board members,*" "*interactions,*" "*structures and leadership,*" and "*decision making culture.*"

These dimensions enable understanding of how board composition, interactions among the board members, the characteristics of the organizational structure, the features of leadership, and the organizational climate (in terms of cohesiveness or degree of conflict) influence board performance and the quality of the board decision-making process.

Despite the reference to the for-profit sector and to the board of directors, the framework provided by Huse (2007) shows great potential for general understanding of human behaviors within organizations. Thus, a tentative approach in adapting Huse's framework to the public sector has been undertaken by first assessing specific literature on the behavioral approach in the public domain. This has been implemented by employing research in the ISI Web of Knowledge research engine. Then, building on the results of this review, the framework proposed by Huse (2007) has been adapted by introducing four dimensions to analyze behaviors within public organizations: *"human resource management," "culture, leadership, and structure," "interactions,"* and *"organizational climate.".*

It has been argued that the way in which human resources are managed, in terms of selection, evaluation assessment, motivation, and incentives, has a great impact on employees' behaviors, not only in the private sector, but also (*especially?*) in the public sector, in which the peculiar characteristics of the tasks to be carried out may engender alienation and turnover.

In the same way, the values and the culture promoted within the organization, and the leadership style adopted may affect positively or negatively employees' behaviors. Here the reference might also be made to managers/superiors adopting behaviors to serve as an example for employees: if a manager does not behave properly, or he/she adopts unethical behavior, it could be a negative example to his/her employees, thus engendering negative imitative behaviors.

Interactions are also important in explaining employees' behaviors. Studies on individual behaviors argue that interactional difficulties often affect individual work performance, and threaten the achievement of full potential in the task to be performed. Employees' interactions are greatly affected by workplace trust: if people trust each other, the willing to work and interact with others will increase. Also power and influence may affect individual behaviors. On the one hand, the possibility of exerting power and influence on other people represents a motivating factor (McClelland, 1961); on the other hand, they could undermine and negatively affect the behaviors of people who have undergone their effects.

The organizational climate represents another key factor determining employees' behaviors. In greater detail, it has been argued that within the organization a high level of cohesiveness, as well as commitment, enables and increases willingness to work with others, while in contrast a high degree of conflict might engender negative behaviors, or people leaving the organization.

Finally, the last section of this chapter has summarized the key features of the behavioral approach as discussed in the other sections, with the aim of explaining how to locate it within the studies on the public sector.

With this aim in mind, the study of Geddes (2012) has been taken as a starting point due to the interesting review of previous models provided by the author. Geddes (2012) analyzed the Public Administration (PA), the New Public Management (NPM), and the Collaborative Public Management (CPM) through 11 management dimensions: performance, accountability, community engagement, values, leadership, employment relations, management tasks, decision-making, structure, processes, and change. Then, the author set out the prevailing model for each management dimension, coming to the conclusion shown in the first three columns of Table 2.2.

In light of the discussion provided in this chapter on the behavioral approach, in Table 2.2 two more columns have been added to highlight what might be the contribution of the behavioral approach to improving on previous models concerning public administration. On this basis, it has been argued that the behavioral approach considers as its main concerns the individual and his/her behaviors as these represent the basis of the organizational analysis. Thus, to solve the problems occurring in organizations – both private and public – an in-depth understanding of the factors driving human behaviors is needed.

In reasoning concerning the 11 management dimensions, the reactions and the possible behaviors that might be adopted by employees should always be considered. In this regard, incentives – both monetary and non-monetary – might help in aligning individual behaviors with the public administration targets, but this also needs increased individual accountability related to low performance or to missed goals.

The main suggestions to be derived from the behavioral approach are that the hierarchy characterizing the bureaucratic approach should be maintained, thus guaranteeing no loss of control over activities, but at the same time increased flexibility should be considered, thus avoiding repetitive tasks and related issues. This may only occur if human resource management, culture, and structures are oriented toward this aim. For instance, a possible solution might emerge by adopting management by project: this could simultaneously increase employees' motivation and accountability, and the degree of organizational flexibility.

# 7. References

Agranoff, R. and McGuire, M., (2003), *Collaborative Public Management.* Washington: George Town University Press.

Alderfer, C.P., (1969), An empirical test of a new theory of human needs, *Organizational Behavior and Human Performance*, vol. 4, no.2, pp. 142-75, doi: 003050736990004X.

Amason, A., (1996), Distinguishing the effects of functional and dysfunctional conflict on strategic decision making: Resolving a paradox for top management teams, *Academy of Management Journal*, vol. 39, no. 1, pp. 123-148. doi: 10.2307/256633.

Anton, C., Camarero, C., and San Jose, R., (2014), Public Employee Acceptance Of New Technological Processes The Case Of An Internal Call Centre, *Public Management Review*, vol. 16, no. 6, pp. 852-875, doi: 10.1080/14719037.2012.758308.

Berg, S.V., (2007). Conflict resolution benchmarking water utility performance. *Public Administration and Development,* vol. 27, pp. 1-11. doi: 10.1002/pad.437.

Blau P.M., (1955), *The dynamics of bureaucracy: a study of interpersonal relations in two Government Agencies*, Chicago: University of Chicago Press.

Boyne, G. and Dahya, J., (2002). Executive succession and the performance of public organizations. *Public Administration*, vol. 80, no. 1, pp. 179-200, doi: 10.1111/1467-9299.00299.

Bozeman B., (2000), *Bureaucracy and Red Tape*, Englewood Cliffs: Prentice Hall.

Bromiley, P., and Cummings, L.L., (1995), Transactions costs in organizations with trust. In R.J. Bies, R.J. Lewicki, and B.L. Sheppard (Eds.) *Research on Negotiations in Organizations*. Greenwich, CT: JAI Press.

Browning, L.D., Beyer, J.M., and Shetler, J.C., (1995), Building cooperation in a competitive industry: SEMATECH and the semiconductor industry, *Academy of Management Journal*, vol. 38, pp. 113-152.

Brundin, E. and Nordqvist N., (2008), Beyond Facts and Figures: The Role of Emotions in Boardroom Dynamics. *Corporate Governance: An International Review*, vol. 16, no. 4, pp. 326-341, doi: 10.1111/j.1467-8683.2008.00688.x.

Brundin, E., (2002), *Emotions in Motion: The Strategic Leader in a Radical Change Process*. Dissertation Series no. 12, Jonkoping International Business School, Jonkoping, Sweden.

Bunderson, J.S., K.M. Sutcliffe. 2003. Management team learning orientation and business unit performance, *Journal of Applied Psychology*, vol. 88, no. 3, pp. 552-560, doi: 10.1037/0021-9010.88.3.552.

Burns, T., (1962), Micropolitics: Mechanisms of Organizational Change. *Administrative Science Quarterly*, 6(3), 257-281, doi: 10.2307/2390703.

Cabral, S., and Lazzarini, S.G., (2015), The "Guarding the Guardians" Problem: An Analysis of the Organizational Performance of an Internal Affairs Division, *Journal Of Public Administration Research And Theory*, vol. 25, no. 3, pp. 797-829, doi: 10.1093/jopart/muu001.

Cadbury A., (2002), *Corporate Governance and Chairmanship. A personal view*, Oxford: Oxford University Press.

Campbell, J.W., (2017), Red tape and transformational leadership: an organizational echelons perspective, *Journal Of Organizational Change Management*, vol. 30, no. 1, pp. 76-90, doi: 10.1108/JOCM-01-2016-0004.

Chen, C.A., and Hsieh, C.W., (2015), Knowledge sharing motivation in the public sector: the role of public service motivation, *International Review Of Administrative Sciences*, vol. 81, no. 4, pp. 812-832, doi: 10.1177/0020852314558032.

Clatworthy, M.A., Mellett, H.J. and Peel, M., (2000), Corporate governance under 'New Public Management': an exemplification. *Corporate Governance: An International Review*, 8(2), pp. 166-176.

Considine M., (2000), Contract Regimes and Reflexive Governance: Comparing Employment Service Reforms in the United Kingdom, the Netherlands, New Zealand and Australia, *Public Administration*, vol. 78, no. 3, pp. 613-638, doi: 10.1111/1467-9299.00221.

Cornforth, C., (2003), *The Governance of Public and Non-Profit Organizations. What Do Boards Do?* London: Routledge.

Cornforth, C., (2012), Nonprofit Governance Research: Limitations of the Focus on Boards and Suggestions for New Directions, *Nonprofit and Voluntary Sector Quarterly*, vol. 41, no. 6, pp. 1116-1135, doi: 10.1177/0899764011427959.

Cornforth, C., and Edwards, C., (1999), Board roles in the strategic management of Non-profit organizations: theory and practice. *Corporate Governance: an International Review*, vol. 7, no. 4, pp. 346-362, doi: 10.1111/1467-8683.00165.

Crewson P.E., (1997), Public-Service Motivation: Building Empirical Evidence of Incidence and Effect, *Journal of Public Administration Research and Theory*, vol. 7, no. 4, pp. 499-518, https://doi.org/10.1093/oxfordjournals.jpart.a024363.

Daft, R.L., and Weick, K.E., (1984), Toward a Model of Organizations as Interpretive Systems. *Academy of Management Review*, vol. 9, no. 2, pp. 284-295, doi: 10.5465/AMR.1984.4277657.

Dahl, R.A., (1957), The concept of power. *Behavioral Science*, vol. 2, no. 2, pp. 201-205.

Dalton, D.R., Daily, C.M., Ellstrand, A.E. and Johnson, J.L. (1998), Meta-analytic reviews of board composition, leadership structure, and financial performance, *Strategic Management Journal*, Vol. 19, no. 3, pp. 269-290, doi: 10.1002/(SICI) 1097-0266(199803)19:3<269::AID-SMJ950>3.0.CO;2-K.

Dalton, D.R., Daily, C.R., Johnson, J.L., and Ellstrand, A.E., (1999), Number of Directors and Financial Performance: A Meta Analysis. *Academy of Management Journal*, vol. 42, no. 6, pp. 674-686, doi: 10.2307/256988.

De Simone, S., Cicotto, G., Pinna, R., and Giustiniano, L., (2016), Engaging public servants Public service motivation, work engagement and work-related stress, *Management Decision*, vol. 54, no. 7, pp. 1569-1594, doi: 10.1108/MD-02-2016-0072.

Deci, E.L., (1975), *Intrinsic motivation*. New York: Plenum.

Deci, E.L., and Ryan, R.M., (1985), *Intrinsic motivation and self-determination in human behavior*. New York: Plenum.

Deci, E.L., Koestner, R., and Ryan, R.M., (1998), *Extrinsic rewards and intrinsic motivation: Clear and reliable effects.* Unpublished manuscript, University of Rochester.

Donaldson, L., (1990), The Ethereal Hand: Organization and Management Theory. *Academy of Management Review*, vol. 15, no. 3, pp. 369-381, doi: 10. 5465/AMR.1990.4308806.

Donaldson, L., and Davis, J.H., (1991), Stewardship Theory or agency theory: CEO governance and shareholder returns, *Australian Journal of Management*, vol. 16, no. 1, pp. 49-64, doi: 10.1177/031289629101600103.

Dopson, S., Stewart, R., and Locock, L., (1999), Regional offices in the new NHS: an analysis of the effects and significance of recent changes. *Public Administration*, vol. 77, no. 1, pp. 91-110, doi: 10.1111/1467-9299.00145.

Dutton, J., and Jackson, S., (1987), Categorizing Strategic Issues: Links to Organizational Action. *Academy of Management Review*, vol. 12, no. 1, pp. 76-90, doi: 10.5465/AMR.1987.4306483.

Erez, M., and Somech, A. 1996. Is group productivity loss the rule or the exception? Effects of culture and group-based motivation. *Academy of Management Journal*, vol. 39, no. 6, pp. 1513-1537, doi: 10.2307/257067.

Finkelstein, S., (1992), Power in top management teams: dimensions, measurement, and validation. *Academy of Management Journal*, vol. 35, no. 3, pp. 505-538, doi: 10.2307/256485.

Finkelstein, S., and Mooney, A.C., (2003), Not the Usual Suspects: How to Use Board Process to Make Boards Better. *Academy of Management Executive*, vol. 17, no. 2, pp. 101-113, doi: 10.5465/AME.2003.10025204.

Finkelstein, S., Hambrick, D.C., and Cannella, A.A., (2008), *Strategic leadership: Theory and research on executives, top management teams, and boards*, Oxford: Oxford University Press.

Forbes, D.P., and Milliken, F.J., (1999), Cognition and corporate governance. Understanding boards of directors as strategic decision-making groups. *Academy of Management Review*, vol. 24, no. 3, pp. 489-505, doi: 10.5465/AMR.1999.2202133.

Gabrielsson, J., and Huse, M., (2004), Context, behaviour and evolution. Challenges in research on boards and governance. *International Studies of Management and Organization*, 34(2), pp. 11-36.

Geddes L., (2012), In Search of Collaborative Public Management, *Public Management Review*, vol. 14, no. 7, pp. 947-966, doi: 10.1080/14719037.2011.650057.

Gerth, H.H. and Mills, C.W., (1948), *From Max Weber: Essays in Sociology.* London: Routledge and Kegan Paul.

Gibson, C.B. and Earley, P.C., (2007), Collective cognition in action: Accumulation, interaction, examination and accommodation in the development and operation of group efficacy beliefs in the workplace. *Academy of Management Review*, vol. 32, no. 2, pp. 438-458, doi: 10.5465/AMR.2007.24351397.

Gnan, L., Hinna, A., and Monteduro F., (2013), Conceptualizing and Researching Governance in Public and Non-Profit Organizations. In G. Gnan, A. Hinna and F. Monteduro (Eds.) *Studies in Public and Non-Profit Governance*. London: Emerald Group Publishing Limited.

Greer, A., and Hoggett, P., (2000), Contemporary governance ad local public spending bodies. *Public Administration*, vol. 78, no. 3, pp. 513-529, doi: 10.1111/1467-9299.00216.

Hackman, J., (1987), The design of work teams, In J. Lorsch (Eds.), *Handbook of organizational behavior*, pp. 314-342, Englewood Cliffs: Prentice-Hall.

Harari, M.B., Herst, D.E.L., Parola, H.R., and Carmona, B.P., (2017), Organizational Correlates of Public Service Motivation: A Meta-analysis of Two Decades of Empirical Research, *Journal Of Public Administration Research And Theory*, vol. 27, no. 1, pp. 68-84, doi: 10.1093/jopart/muw056.

Hendry, K., and Kiel, G.C., (2004), The Role of the Board in Firm Strategy: Integrating Agency and Organizational Control Perspectives, *Corporate Governance: An International Review*, vol. 12, no. 4, pp. 500-520, doi: 10.1111/j.1467-8683.2004.00390.x.

Hermalin, B.E., and Weisbach, M.S., (1991), The Effects of Board Composition and Direct Incentives on Firm Performance, *Financial Management*, vol. 20, no. 4, pp. 101-112.

Higashide, H., and Birley, S., (2002), The consequences of conflict between the venture capitalist and the entrepreneurial team in the United Kingdom from the perspective of the venture capitalist, *Journal of Business Venturing*, vol. 17, no. 1, pp. 59-82, doi: 10.1016/S0883-9026(00)00057-4.

Higgs, D., (2003), *Review of the Role and Effectiveness of Non-Executive Directors*. London: Department of Trade and Industry.

Hillman, A.J., and Dalziel, T., (2003), Boards of Directors and Firm Performance: Integrating Agency and Resource Dependence Perspectives, *Academy of Management Review*, vol. 28, no. 3, pp. 383-396, doi: 10.5465/AMR.2003.10196729.

Hinna A., De Nito E., Mangia G., Scarozza D., Tomo A., (2014), "Advancing Public Governance Research: Individual and Collective Dynamics in and Around the Boardroom", In Hinna A., Gnan L., Monteduro F., (eds.), Mechanisms, Roles and Consequences of Governance: Emerging Issues, pp. 3-39, London: Emerald Publishing.

Hinna, A., and Scarozza, D., (2015), A behavioral perspective for governing bodies: Processes and conflicts in public organizations, *International Studies of Management & Organization*, vol. 45, no. 1, pp. 43-59, doi: 10.1080/00208825.2015.1005996.

Hinna, A., Mangia, G., De Nito, E., (2010), Board of director within public organizations: A literature review, *International Journal of Business Governance and Ethics*, vol. 5, no. 3, pp. 131-156, doi: 10.1504/IJBGE.2010.033343.

Homberg, F., McCarthy, D., and Tabvuma, V., (2015), A Meta-Analysis of the Relationship between Public Service Motivation and Job Satisfaction, *Public Administration Review*, vol. 75, no. 5, pp. 711-722, doi:10.1111/puar.12423.

Hood C. (1991), A Public Management for all Seasons?, *Public Administration*, vol. 69, no. 1, pp. 3-39. doi: 10.1111/j.1467-9299.1991.tb00778.x.

Hood, C., James, O., and Scott, C., (2000), Regulation of government: Has it increased, is it increasing, should it be diminished? *Public Administration*, *78*(2), pp. 283-304, doi: 10.1111/1467-9299.00206.

Horwitz, S.K., and Horwitz, I.B., (2007), The Effects of Team Diversity on Team Outcomes: A Meta-Analytic Review of Team Demography, *Journal of Management*, vol. 33, no. 6, pp. 987-1015, doi: 10.1177/0149206307308587.

Hosmer, L.R.T., (1995), Trust: The connecting link between organizational theory and philosophical ethics, *Academy of Management Review*, vol. 20, no. 2, pp. 379-403, doi: 10.5465/AMR.1995.9507312923.

Huber, G.P., and Lewis, K. 2010. Cross-understanding: Implications for group cognition and performance, *Academy of Management Review*, vol. 35, no. 1, pp. 6-26.

Huberts L.W.J.C., Kaptein M., Lasthuizen K., (2007), A study of the impact of three leadership styles on integrity violations committed by police officers, *Policing: An International Journal of Police Strategies & Management*, Vol. 30, no. 4, pp. 587-607, doi: 10.1108/13639510710833884.

Huse M., (1998), Researching the dynamics of board-stakeholder relations. *Long-Range Planning*, vol. 31, no. 2, pp. 218-226, doi: 10.1016/S0024-6301(98) 00006-5.

Huse, M., (1990), Board composition in small enterprises. *Entrepreneurship and Regional Development*, vol. 2, no. 4, pp. 363-373, doi: 10.1080/08985629000000023.

Huse, M., (2000), Boards of Directors in SMEs: a Review and Research Agenda. *Entrepreneurship and Regional Development*, vol. 12, no. 4, pp. 271-290, doi: 10.1080/08985620050177912.

Huse, M., (2007), *Boards, Governance and Value Creation*, Cambridge: Cambridge University Press.

Huse, M., and Eide, D., (1996), Stakeholder Management and the Avoidance of Corporate Control". *Business and Society*, vol. 35, no. 2, pp. 211-243, doi: 10.1177/000765039603500204.

Huse, M., and Solberg, A.G., (2006), Gender-related boardroom dynamics: how women make and can make contributions on corporate boards. *Women in Management Review*, vol. 21, no. 2, pp. 113-130, doi: 10.1108/09649420610650693.

Hyndman, N., and Eden, R., (2001), Rational management, performance targets and executive agencies: views from agency chief executives in Northern Ireland. *Public Administration*, vol. 79, no. 3, pp. 579-598, doi: 10.1111/1467-9299. 00270.

Jehn, K.A., (1997), A Qualitative Analysis of Conflict Types and Dimensions in Organizational Groups. *Administrative Science Quarterly,* vol. 42, no. 3, pp. 530-557, doi: 0001-8392/97/4203-0530.

Jensen, M.C., (1993), The modern industrial revolution, exit, and the failure of internal control system. *Journal of Finance*, vol. 48, no. 3, pp. 831-880, doi: 10.1111/j.1540-6261.1993.tb04022.x.

Johannisson, B., and Huse, M., (2000), Recruiting outside board members in the small family business: an ideological change. *Entrepreneurship and Regional Development*, vol. 12, no. 4, pp. 353-378, doi: 10.1080/08985620050177958.

Johnson, G., Melin, L., and Whittington, R., (2003), Micro strategy and strategizing: towards and activity based view. *Journal of Management Studies*, vol. 40, no. 1, pp. 3-20, doi: 10.1111/1467-6486.t01-2-00002.

Jonnergard, K., and Stafsudd, A., (2011), The making of active boards in Swedish public companies. *Journal of Management and Governance,* vol. 15, no. 1, pp. 123-155, doi: 10.1007/s10997-009-9120-y.

Jorgensen, T.B., (1999), The Public Sector in an in-between time: searching for new public values. *Public Administration*, vol. 77, no. 3, pp. 565-584, doi: 10.1111/1467-9299.00168.

Kahnemann D., (2011), *Thinking fast and slow*, New York: Macmillan.

Kickert, W.J.M., Klijn, E.H., and Koppenjan, J.F.M., (1997), *Managing Complex Networks: Strategies for the Public Sector*. London: Sage.

Kim, T., Henderson, A.C., and Eom, T.H., (2015), At the front line: examining the effects of perceived job significance, employee commitment, and job involvement on public service motivation, *International Review Of Administrative Sciences*, vol. 81, no. 4, pp. 713-733, doi: 10.1177/0020852314558028.

Kirkbride, J., and Letza, S., (2003), Corporate governance and gatekeeper liability: the lessons from public authorities. *Corporate Governance: An International Review*, vol. 11, no. 3, pp. 262-271, doi: 10.1111/1467-8683.00323.

Klijn, E., and Skelcher, C., (2007), Democracy and governance networks: Compatible or not?. *Public Administration*, vol. 85, no. 3, pp. 587-608, doi: 10.1111/j.1467-9299.2007.00662.x.

Ko, J., and Hur, S., (2014), The Impacts of Employee Benefits, Procedural Justice, and Managerial Trustworthiness on Work Attitudes: Integrated Understanding Based on Social Exchange Theory, *Public Administration Review*, vol. 74, no. 2, pp. 176-187, doi: 10.1111/puar.12160.

Kolthoff, E., (2016), Integrity Violations, White-Collar Crime, and Violations of Human Rights: Revealing the Connection, *Public Integrity*, vol. 18, no. 4, pp. 396-418, doi: 10.1080/10999922.2016.1172933.

Korsgaard, M.A., Schweiger D.M., and Sapienza, H.J., (1995), Building commitment, attachment, and trust in strategic decision making teams: the role of procedural justice. *Academy of Management Journal*, vol. 38, no. 1, pp. 60-85, doi: doi: 10.2307/256728.

Kosnik, B., (1990), Effects of board demography and directors incentives on corporate greenmail decisions. *Academy of Management Journal,* vol. 33, no. 1, pp. 129-150, doi: 10.2307/256355.

Larson, A., (1992), Network dyads in entrepreneurial settings: a study of the governance of exchange relationships. *Administrative Science Quarterly*, vol. 37, no. 1, pp. 76-104, doi: 10.2307/2393534.

Lawrence, B., (1997), The black box of organizational demography. *Organization Science*, vol. 8, no. 4, pp. 1-22, doi: 10.1287/orsc.8.1.1.

Leblanc, R., and Gillies, J., (2005), *Inside the Boardroom: How Boards Really Work and the Coming Revolution in Corporate Governance*. Hoboken, NJ: John Wiley & Sons.

Locke, E.A., and Latham, G.P., (1990), A theory of goal setting and task performance. Englewood Cliffs, NJ: Prentice-Hall.

Lowndes, V., and Wilson, D., (2003), Balancing revisability and robustness? A new institutionalist perspective on local government modernization. *Public Administration*, vol. 81, no. 2, pp. 275-298, doi: 10.1111/1467-9299.00346.

Luhmann, N., (1988), Familiarity, confidence, trust: problems and alternatives. In D. Gambetta (Eds.) *Trust: Making and Breaking Cooperative Relations*. Oxford: Basil Blackwell.

Lukes, S., (1974), *Power: a radical view*. London: The Macmillan Press Ltd.

Maslow A., (1954), *Motivation and Personality*, New York: Harper.

McAllister, D.J., (1995), Affect and cognitive based trust as foundation for interpersonal cooperation in organizations. *Academy of Management Journal*, vol. 38, no. 1, pp. 24-59, doi: 10.2307/256727.

McClelland D.C., (1961), *The Achieving Society*. New York: Free Press.

McNulty, T., and Pettigrew, A., (1999), Strategists on the board. *Organizational Studies*, vol. 20, no. 1, pp. 47-74, doi: 10.1177/0170840699201003.

Melone, N., (1994), Reasoning in the executive suite: The influence of role/ex perience based expertise on decision processes of corporate executives. *Organization Science*, vol. 5, no. 3, pp. 438-455, doi: 10.1287/orsc.5.3.438.

Michels, R., (1962), *Political Parties: A sociological Study of the Oligarchical Tendencies of Modern Democracy*. New York: Collier.

Midttun, A., and Kamfjord, S., (1999), Energy and environmental governance under ecological modernization: a comparative analysis of Nordic countries. *Public Administration*, vol. 77, no. 49, pp. 873-895, doi: 10.1111/1467-9299.00184.

Milliken, F.J., and Martins, L., (1996), Searching for common threads: understanding the multiple effects of diversity in organizational groups. *Academy of Management Review*, vol. 21, no. 2, pp. 402-433, doi: 10.5465/AMR.1996.9605060217.

Mintzberg, H., (1979), *The Structuring of Organizations*, Englewood Cliffs: Prentice Hall.

Mintzberg, H., (1983), *Power in and around organizations*. Englewood Cliffs: Prentice Hall.

Monks, R.A.G. and Minow, N., (2004), *Corporate Governance*. Oxford: Basil Balckwell.

Moynihan, D.P., and Pandey, S. K., (2007), The Role of Organizations in Fostering Public Service Motivation, *Public Administration Review*, vol. 67, no. 1, pp. 40-53. doi:10.1111/j.1540-6210.2006.00695.x.

Nahapiet and Goshal, (1998), Social Capital, Intellectual Capital, and the Organizational Advantage, *Academy of Management Review*, vol. 23, no. 2, pp. 242-266, doi: 10.5465/AMR.1998.533225.

Narayanan, V.K., and Fahey, L., (1982), The Micro-Politics of Strategy Formulation. *Academy of Management Review*, vol. 7, no. 1, pp. 25-34, doi: 10.5465/AMR.1982.4285432.

Nielsen, V.L., (2015), Personal Attributes and Institutions: Gender and the Behavior of Public Employees. Why Gender Matters to not only "Gendered Policy

Areas", *Journal Of Public Administration Research And Theory*, vol. 25, no. 4, pp. 1005-1029, doi: 10.1093/jopart/muu019.

Ocasio, W., (1994), Political dynamics and the circulation of power: CEO succession in US industrial corporations 1960-1990. *Administrative Science Quarterly*, vol. 39, no. 2, pp. 285-312, doi: 10.2307/2393237.

Ocasio, W., (1999), Institutionalised Action and Corporate Governance: The Reliance on Rules of CEO Succession. *Administrative Science Quarterly*, vol. 44, no. 2, pp. 384-416, doi: 10.2307/2667000.

Oldenhof, L., Postma, J., and Putters, K., (2014), On Justification Work: How Compromising Enables Public Managers to Deal with Conflicting Values, *Public Administration Review*, vol. 74, no. 1, pp. 52-63, doi: 10.1111/puar.12153.

Osborne, D. and Gaebler, T., (1992), *Reinventing Government. How the Entrepreneurial Spirit is Transforming the Public Sector*. New York: Penguin Books.

Osterloh, M., and Frey, B.S., (2004), Corporate Governance for crooks? The case for corporate virtue. In A. Grandori (Eds.) *Corporate Governance and Firm Organization: Microfoundations and Structural Forms*. Oxford: Oxford University Press.

Patton, A., and Baker, J.C., (1987), Why Won't Directors Rock the Boat? *Harvard Business Review*, vol. 65, pp. 10-18.

Pearce, J.A., II, and Zahra, S.A., (1991), The Relative Power of CEOs and Boards of Directors: Associations with Corporate Performance. *Strategic Management Journal,* vol. 12, no. 2, pp. 135-153, doi: 10.1002/smj.4250120205.

Perry, J.L., (1996), Measuring Public Service Motivation: An Assessment of Construct Reliability and Validity, *Journal of Public Administration Research and Theory*, vol. 6, no. 1, pp. 5-22, https://doi.org/10.1093/oxfordjournals.jpart.a024303.

Perry, J.L., (1997), Antecedents of Public Service Motivation, *Journal of Public Administration Research and Theory*, vol. 7, no. 2, pp. 181-197, https://doi.org/10.1093/oxfordjournals.jpart.a024345.

Pettigrew, A., (1992), On Studying Managerial Elites. *Strategic Management Journal*, vol. 13, SI 2, pp. 163-182, doi: 10.1002/smj.4250130911.

Pettigrew, A., and McNulty, T., (1995), Power and Influences in and around the Boardroom. *Human Relations*, vol. 48, no. 8, pp. 845-873, doi: 10.1177/00187 2679504800802.

Pettigrew, A.M., and McNulty T., (1998), Sources and uses of power in the boardroom. *European Journal of Work and Organizational Psychology*, vol. 7, no. 2, pp. 197-214, doi: 10.1080/135943298398871.

Pfeffer, J., Salancik G.R., (1978), *The External Control of Organizations: A Resource Dependence Perspective*. New York: Harper and Row.

Piatak, J.S., (2015), Altruism by Job Sector: Can Public Sector Employees Lead the Way in Rebuilding Social Capital? *Journal Of Public Administration Research And Theory*, vol. 25, no. 3, pp. 877-900, doi: 10.1093/jopart/muu013.

Ravasi, D. and Zattoni, A., (2006) Exploring the political side of board involvement in strategy: A study of mixed-ownership institutions, *Journal of Management Studies*, vol. 43, no. 8, pp. 1671-1702, doi: 10.1111/j.1467-6486.2006.00659.x.

Ring, P.S., (1996), Fragile and resilient trust and their roles in economic exchange. *Business and Society*, vol. 35, no. 2, pp. 148-175, doi: 10.1177/0007650396 03500202.

Roberts, J., McNulty T., and Stiles P., (2005), Beyond Agency Conceptions of the Work of the Non-Executive Director: Creating Accountability in the Boardroom. *British Journal of Management*, vol. 16, SI 1, pp. S5-S26, doi: 10.1111/j. 1467-8551.2005.00444.x.

Sanderson, I., (2002), Performance management, evaluation and learning in 'Modern' Local Government. *Public Administration*, vol. 79, no. 2, 297-313, doi: 10.1111/1467-9299.00257.

Sapienza, H.J., Korsgaard, M.A., Goulet, P.K., and Hoogendam, J.P., (2000), Effects of Agency Risks and Procedural Justice on Board Processes in Venture Capital-backed Firms. *Entrepreneurship & Regional Development*, vol. 12, no. 4, pp. 331-351, doi: 10.1080/08985620050177949.

Shropshire, C., (2010), The role of the interlocking director and board receptivity in the diffusion of practices, *Academy of Management Review*, vol. 35, no. 2, pp. 246-264.

Siciliano, R., (2002), The Nixon Pay Board – A Public Administration Disaster. *Public Administration Review*, vol. 62, no. 3, pp. 791-803, doi: 10.1111/1540-6210.00187

Smith, K.G., Smith, K.A., Olian, J.D., Sims, H.P., O'Bannen, D.P., and Scully, J.A., (1994), Top management team demography and processes: the role of integration and communication. *Administrative Science Quarterly*, vol. 39, no. 3, pp. 412-438, doi: 10.2307/2393297.

Smith, M., and Beazley, M., (2000), Progressive regimes, partnerships and the involvement of local communities: a framework for evaluation. *Public Administration*, vol. 78, no. 4, pp. 855-878, doi: 10.1111/1467-9299.00234.

Sonnenfeld, J.A., (2002), What makes greats boards great. *Harvard Business Review*, vol. 80, no. 9, pp. 106-113.

Steel, P., and Konig, C.J., (2006), Integrating theories of motivation. *Academy of Management Review*, vol. 31, no. 4, pp. 889-913, doi: 10.5465/AMR.2006.22527462

Stiles, P., and Taylor, B., (2001), *Boards at Work: How Directors View Their Roles and Responsibilities*. Oxford: Oxford University Press.

Sullivan, H., Barnes M. and Matka, E., (2006), Collaborative *Capacity* and strategies in area-based initiatives. *Public Administration*, vol. 84, no. 2, pp. 289-310, doi: 10.1111/j.1467-9299.2006.00003.x.

Svara, J.H., (2014), Who Are the Keepers of the Code? Articulating and Upholding Ethical Standards in the Field of Public Administration, *Public Administration Review*, vol. 74, no. 5, pp. 561-569, doi: 10.1111/puar.12230.

Taylor, F.W., (1947), *Scientific Management*. New York: Harper and Row.

Thomas, J.B., Shankster, L.J., and Mathieu, J.E., (1994), Antecedents to Organizational Issue Interpretation: The Roles of Single-Level, Cross-Level, and Content Cues. *Academy of Management Journal*, vol. 37, no. 5, pp. 1252-1284, doi: 10.2307/256672.

Tomo A., Scarozza D., Hinna A., De Nito E., and Mangia G., (2016), "Exploring Board Conflicts in Public Organizations: Sources, Nature, and Effects", In Gnan L., Hinna A., Monteduro F., (eds.) *Governance and Performance in Public and Non-Profit Organizations*, pp. 53-74, London: Emerald Publishing.

Tummers, L., Bekkers, V., van Thiel, S., and Steijn, B., (2014), The Effects of Work Alienation and Policy Alienation on Behavior of Public Employees, *Administration & Society*, vol. 47, no. 5, pp. 596-617, doi: 10.1177/0095399714555748.

Van Witteloostuijn, A., Esteve, M., and Boyne, G., (2017), Public Sector Motivation ad fonts: Personality Traits as Antecedents of the Motivation to Serve the Public Interest, *Journal Of Public Administration Research And Theory*, vol. 27, no. 1, pp. 20-35, doi: 10.1093/jopart/muw027.

Vandenabeele, W., Brewer, G.A., and Ritz, A., (2014), Past, Present, And Future Of Public Service Motivation Research, *Public Administration*, vol. 92, no. 4, pp. 779-789, doi: 10.1111/padm.12136.

West, W.F., and Durant, R., (2000), Merit, management and neutral competence: lessons from the US merit systems protection board. *Public Administration Review*, vol. 60, no. 2, pp. 111-122, doi: 10.1111/0033-3352.00070.

Westphal, J.D., and Zajac, E.J., (1998), The symbolic management of stockholders: Corporate governance reforms and shareholder reactions, *Administrative Science Quarterly*, vol. 43, no. 1, pp. 127-153, doi: 10.2307/2393593.

Wright, B.E., (2015), The Science of Public Administration: Problems, Presumptions, Progress, and Possibilities, *Public Administration Review*, vol. 75, no. 6, pp. 795-805, doi: 10.1111/puar.12468.

Wynen, J., and Verhoest, K., (2015), Do NPM-Type Reforms Lead to a Cultural Revolution Within Public Sector Organizations? *Public Management Review*, vol. 17, no. 3, pp. 356-379, doi: 10.1080/14719037.2013.841459.

Yukl, G., (1998), *Leadership in Organizations*. Englewood Cliffs, NJ: Prentice-Hall.

Zajac, E.J., and Westphal, J.D., (1996), Director reputation, CEO-board power, and the dynamics of board interlocks. *Administrative Science Quarterly,* vol. 41, no. 3, pp. 507-29, doi: 10.5465/AMBPP.1996.4980568.

Chapter 3

# BUREAUCRACY, POST-BUREAUCRACY, OR ANARCHY? EVIDENCE FROM THE ITALIAN SETTING

SUMMARY: 1. Introduction. – 2. Research design and hypotheses. – 3. Results. – 3.1. Descriptive statistics. – 3.2. Correlation test. – 3.3. Linear regression. – 3.4. Answers to the research hypotheses. – 3.5. Focus groups: solutions proposed by the participants. – 4. Discussion. – 5. Final remarks and research limits. – 6. References.

## 1. Introduction

Starting from the considerations made in the previous chapters, this chapter will explore dimensions such as individual behaviors, personal qualities, and interpersonal relationships in the public service environment with a specific focus on the Italian setting.

In the first it has been argued that the literature since 1991 mainly concentrated on Anglo-Saxon countries (Alexander et al., 2011; Callanan, 2005; Carey and Matthews, 2017; Charlesworth et al., 1996; Cloutier et al., 2016; Considine, 2000; Currie and Procter, 2005; Entwistle and Martin, 2005; Finn et al., 2010; Gatenby et al., 2015; Germov, 2005; Kane and Patapan, 2006; Kelly, 2006; Kinder, 2012; Kirkpatrick and Ackroyd, 2003; Kirkpatrick, 1999; Kitchener and Gask, 2003; Knott and Miller, 2006; Knott, 2011; Kothari and Handscombe, 2007; Learmonth, 2005; Martin, 2011; McGivern et al., 2015; Meier and Bohte, 2001; Orr and Vince, 2009; Pollitt, 2009; Rothstein and Downer, 2012; Williams et al., 2016), while less attention has been devoted to the countries in the Continental Europe (Bang, 2004; Berg, 2006; Bode and Dent, 2014; Currie et al., 2011; De Boer et al., 2007; Fotaki, 2011; Geddes, 2012; Gourdin and Schepers, 2009; Hammerschmid and Meyer, 2005; Jeffares and Skelcher, 2011; Kickert, 2005; Lega and DePietro, 2005; Lehmann Nielsen, 2006; Martin et al., 2009; Meyer et al., 2014; Meynhardt and Diefenbach, 2012; Noordegraaf and De Wit, 2012; Raadschelders, 1995; Seibel, 2010; Vinot, 2014; Voets et al., 2015), especially to those in the Southern area (Correia and Denis, 2016; Kickert, 2005, 2011; Lega and DePietro, 2005; Magone, 2011; Ongaro, 2006), despite their peculiarities.

From the analysis of the literature two main gaps emerge. First, there are no studies analyzing the features of the organizational model and the activities carried out by public servants in the modern public administrations. The attention has been always paid to the rules driving the PA, following the bureaucratic model; then on the performance, following the NPM reforms; finally, on the search for collaboration, networks, and partnerships in light of the NPG approach.

Second, there is a lack of attention towards the countries in the Southern Europe. These countries present interesting and peculiar characteristics due to historical, cultural, and political differences respect to the Anglo-Saxon and other Continental European countries.

Thus, the research questions driving the analysis in this chapter are the following: *Which organizational features characterize modern public administrations? What factors influence the predominance of different models? What aspects characterize the activities carried out by public servants?*

By employing questionnaires and interviews with 156 Italian public managers, officers and employees, issues regarding job characteristics, leadership/managerial style, human resource management (personal motivation and incentives), organizational climate, individual targets, and public administration of affiliation targets will be analyzed and discussed. These issues are key points in answering the research question and achieving the aim of understanding which organizational features characterize Italian public administrations.

Additionally, the discussion of these issues may support the development of solutions to improve operational management and perform a better change management in the public sector: if the awareness about the above-mentioned dimensions is also raised in the public sector domain, it will be possible to develop better organizational models that balance the satisfaction of public stakeholders and the respect of the principles of performance and efficiency.

The chapter is structured as follows. Section 2 sets the research design and presents the hypotheses driving the analysis. In section 3, for reasons of clarity, the results are presented in five subsections relative to: the descriptive statistics; the results of the correlation test; the results of the linear regression; the specific answers to the research hypotheses, and the results from the face-to-face interviews. Section 4 discusses the results, while section 5 presents the final remarks and research limitations.

## 2. Research design and hypotheses

The analysis relies upon a mixed method approach based on the administering of questionnaires and on focus groups with participants to better catch the nuances emerging from their replies to the questionnaire. The structured questionnaire has been administered to 156 Italian public managers, officers and employees. The questionnaires and interviews were administered during different training courses that the participants were attending on issues regarding the public administration.

In more detail, the questionnaire was structured in thirteen questions concerning age, the public administration of affiliation, the job qualification (manager/officer/employee), the number of years in service, the priority of the PA of affiliation, the job horizontal specialization degree (four-point scale), the job vertical specialization degree (four-point scale), the formalization degree (six-point scale) within the PA of affiliation, the managerial style perceived within the PA of affiliation (coercive/participative/democratic), the degree of personal motivation (six-point scale), the conflict degree (six-point scale) within the PA, the personal target and solutions to improve personal motivation.

Relative to the specialization degree, it was explained to the participants that a high degree of specialization (both horizontal and vertical) corresponds to a low number of tasks, and to a low degree of control over the job.

Regarding the managerial style, it is worth noting that a fourth category has been added to the three categories reported within the questionnaire (coercive/participative/democratic), since numerous participants, while completing the questionnaires, asked whether it was possible to add the term "anarchy," explaining that, within their administration of affiliation, they perceived a climate and a method of managing that could be defined more accurately as anarchy.

The face-to-face interviews aimed to gain a better understanding of which solutions the participants have in mind to solve the main issues (specialization, complexity, formalization, conflict and motivation) related to their job, to their administration's characteristics and to overcoming bureaucracy's negative aspects. In greater detail questions were related to interventions in the formalization degree, specialization degree, conflict resolution, desired managerial style, solutions to improve employees' motivation and solutions to overcome bureaucracy's hurdles.

The focus on the Italian setting is due to the lack of attention emerging from the literature first to those countries in the southern part of Europe and then to the specificity of the Italian context, characterized by a high degree of prevalence of formality on the substance, typically featuring the bureaucratic model. On this ground, the first hypothesis to be tested is:

*H1: Italian public administrations are still rooted in a bureaucratic model.*

Consequently, the job characteristics should be imprinted with high specialization, both horizontal and vertical, high formalization, and low employee motivation. Indeed, here it is considered what stated by Merton (1940) on his belief that bureaucrats took pride in their craft, thus it is expected a high motivation degree. In turn, personal motivation should depend positively on high degrees of specialization, formalization, on democratic and participative managerial styles, and negatively on the degree of conflict. Thus, the second hypothesis is:

*H2a: Jobs' characteristics present high standardization (both horizontal and vertical), high formalization, and high motivation*

and

*H2b: Personal motivation depends positively on a high specialization degree (both horizontal and vertical), high formalization degree, the managerial style, and negatively on a high conflict degree*

Additionally, the managerial style in line with these characteristics should be mainly coercive. Thus, the third hypothesis is proposed as follows:

*H3: The managerial styles adopted mainly present the characteristics of a coercive approach.*

## Data analysis

To test these hypotheses and to answer the research question, descriptive statistics will be supported by a Pearson's correlation test and a linear regression performed with the statistics program SPSS 16.0.

## Pearson's correlation test

A correlation test was conducted between all the variables. Specifically, the variables were interpreted as follows.

- Age: less than 30 = 1; from 30 to 40 = 2; from 40 to 50 = 3; over 50 = 4;
- Horizontal specialization degree: from 1 (low) to 4 (high);
- Vertical specialization degree: from 1 (low) to 4 (high);
- Formalization degree: from 0 (null) to 5 (very high);
- Personal motivation: from 0 (null) to 5 (very high);
- Conflict degree: from 0 (null) to 5 (very high);
- Job qualification, public administration of affiliation, public administration's priority, managerial styles, and solutions to improve motivation were treated as polychotomous variables.

## Linear regression

Linear regression was performed to test the dependence of personal motivation on the specialization degree, the complexity degree, the formalization degree, the conflict degree, and the managerial style.

In this case, the variables were labeled as follows:

- Horizontal specialization degree: from 1 (low) to 4 (high);
- Vertical specialization degree: from 1 (low) to 4 (high);
- Formalization degree: from 0 (null) to 5 (very high);
- Personal motivation: from 0 (null) to 5 (very high);
- Conflict degree: from 0 (null) to 5 (very high);
- Managerial style: anarchy = 0; coercive = 1; democratic = 2; participative = 3.

## 3. Results

This section is structured as follows: subsection 3.1 provides the descriptive statistics of the sample; subsection 3.2 presents the results from the correlation test; subsection 3.3 provides the results from the linear regression; subsection 3.4 provides the answers to the specific research hypotheses; and subsection 3.5 contains the results from the interviews.

### 3.1. Descriptive statistics

*Participants' personal information*

The observed sample shows that most of the participants are aged from 40 to 50 (nearly 80%) (see Table 3.1) and they have mostly been in service for 10-20 years (44%) (see Table 3.2).

**Table 3.1.** Participants' age.

| Participants' age | N | % |
|---|---|---|
| Under 30 years old | 9 | 6% |
| Between 30 and 40 years old | 15 | 10% |
| Between 40 and 50 years old | 123 | 79% |
| Over 50 years old | 9 | 5% |
| **TOTAL** | **156** | **100%** |

**Table 3.2.** Years in service.

| Years in service | N | % |
|---|---|---|
| Less than 5 years | 9 | 6% |
| Between 5 and 10 years | 15 | 10% |
| Between 10 and 20 years | 69 | 44% |
| More than 20 years | 63 | 40% |
| **TOTAL** | **156** | **100%** |

Most of the participants come from local (48%) and central government (27%) institutions (see Table 3.3). More than half of them are officers (56%) and 31% are employees, while only 13% are managers (see Table 3.4).

**Table 3.3.** PA of affiliation.

| PA of affiliation | N | % |
|---|---|---|
| Local government | 75 | 48% |
| Central government | 42 | 27% |
| Health and social care | 9 | 6% |
| Education | 18 | 11% |
| Research institute | 9 | 6% |
| Social insurance institute | 3 | 2% |
| **TOTAL** | **156** | **100%** |

**Table 3.4.** Job qualifications.

| Job qualifications | N | % |
|---|---|---|
| Manager | 21 | 13% |
| Officer | 87 | 56% |
| Employee | 48 | 31% |
| **TOTAL** | **156** | **100%** |

## *Job characteristics*

Following Mintzberg (1979) regarding job characteristics, the participants were asked to indicate their job specialization degree, both horizontal (the number of tasks to perform) and vertical (the degree of control over the job). The following tables show the horizontal (Table 3.5) and the vertical (Table 3.6) specialization degree.

**Table 3.5.** Horizontal specialization degree.

| Horizontal specialization degree | N | % |
|---|---|---|
| 1 (Low) | 3 | 2% |
| 2 (Relatively low) | 6 | 4% |
| 3 (Relatively high) | 111 | 71% |
| 4 (High) | 36 | 23% |
| TOTAL | 156 | 100% |

**Table 3.6.** Vertical specialization degree.

| Vertical specialization degree | N | % |
|---|---|---|
| 1 (Low) | 0 | 0% |
| 2 (Relatively low) | 9 | 6% |
| 3 (Relatively high) | 105 | 67% |
| 4 (High) | 42 | 27% |
| TOTAL | 156 | 100% |

The tables show that both horizontal specialization and vertical specialization are "relatively high" (71% and 67%) or "high" (23% and 27%). These data become even more interesting when cumulating the percentages of degrees 3 and 4, which cover 94% of cases.

Tables 3.7 and 3.8 show the level of personal motivation and solutions to improve employees' motivation.

**Table 3.7.** Personal motivation.

| Personal motivation | N | % |
|---|---|---|
| 0 (Insufficient) | 3 | 2% |
| 1 (Low) | 9 | 6% |
| 2 (Relatively low) | 24 | 15% |
| 3 (Relatively high) | 63 | 40% |
| 4 (High) | 30 | 19% |
| 5 (Very high) | 27 | 18% |
| TOTAL | 156 | 100% |

**Table 3.8.** Solutions to improve personal motivation.

| Solutions to improve personal motivation | N | % |
|---|---|---|
| Monetary incentives | 51 | 33% |
| Non-monetary incentives | 12 | 8% |
| Career development | 66 | 42% |
| Developing informal and participative leadership | 24 | 15% |
| Superiors adopting behaviors to set an example | 3 | 2% |
| TOTAL | 156 | 100% |

Table 3.7 shows "relatively high" motivation among 40% of the participants and "high" motivation among 19% of the participants. Indeed, Table 3.8 shows that most of the participants gave greater importance to career development (42%) and monetary incentives (33%) as solutions to improve personal motivation. Only 15% reported the development of informal leadership, 8% indicated non-monetary incentives and just 2% recognized a positive influence on motivation in superiors adopting behaviors to set an example for their employees.

## Organizational characteristics

The organizational characteristics, analyzed through the questionnaire, are related to the formalization degree, the priority of the PA, the managerial style and the conflict degree.

Table 3.9 shows the results relating to the formalization degree: in this case, surprisingly, the balance needle is more oriented towards a low degree (38% "relatively low"; 52% when cumulating "null", "low" and "relatively low"). There are nevertheless high percentages of "relatively high" (31%) and "high" (15%).

**Table 3.9.** Formalization degree.

| Formalization degree | N | % |
|---|---|---|
| 0 (Null) | 6 | 4% |
| 1 (Low) | 15 | 10% |
| 2 (Relatively low) | 60 | 38% |
| 3 (Relatively high) | 48 | 31% |
| 4 (High) | 24 | 15% |
| 5 (Excessive) | 3 | 2% |
| TOTAL | 156 | 100% |

Table 3.10 contains the answers to the question "what do you think is the priority of your PA of affiliation?" The results interestingly show that the priority of the PA is represented in 68% of the cases by "respecting the rules.".

**Table 3.10.** Public administration's priority.

| Public administration's priority | N | % |
|---|---|---|
| Respecting the rules | 105 | 68% |
| Improving economic and financial performance | 27 | 17% |
| Satisfying public stakeholders | 24 | 15% |
| **TOTAL** | **156** | **100%** |

Another question asked the participants to indicate which managerial style is mainly adopted within their PA of affiliation. There were three possible answers: coercive, participative, and democratic. As previously highlighted, during the questionnaire submission, numerous participants asked whether it was possible to add the term "anarchy"; thus, after the first ten responses, the term was included in the subsequent questionnaire submissions. Table 3.11 shows the final results: anarchy resulted as the most selected style (33%), while the second choice was "coercive" (31%).

**Table 3.11.** Managerial styles.

| Managerial styles | N | % |
|---|---|---|
| Anarchy | 51 | 33% |
| Coercive | 48 | 31% |
| Participative | 42 | 27% |
| Democratic | 15 | 10% |
| **TOTAL** | **156** | **100%** |

Finally, to obtain a proxy for the organizational climate, the participants were asked to indicate the degree of conflict within their PA of affiliation. Table 3.12 shows that more than half of the participants reported a "relatively high" (52%) degree of conflict, and another relevant percentage (29%) reported a "high" level of conflict.

**Table 3.12.** Conflict degree.

| Conflict degree | N | % |
|---|---|---|
| 0 (Null) | 0 | 0% |
| 1 (Low) | 3 | 2% |
| 2 (Relatively low) | 18 | 11% |
| 3 (Relatively high) | 81 | 52% |
| 4 (High) | 45 | 29% |
| 5 (Very high) | 9 | 6% |
| **TOTAL** | **156** | **100%** |

## *Personal targets*

The final question was intended to understand the personal target of the participants. The possible options suggested were: respecting the rules, finding solutions to citizens' problems, reaching PA targets and reaching individual targets. Table 3.13 shows that the main target is represented by "reaching PA targets" (35%), followed by "finding solutions to citizens' problems" (33%) and "respecting the rules" (29%). Indeed, "reaching individual targets" represents only 4%.

**Table 3.13.** Personal targets.

| Personal targets | N | % |
|---|---|---|
| Finding solutions to citizens' problems | 51 | 33% |
| Respecting the rules | 45 | 29% |
| Reaching PA targets | 54 | 35% |
| Reaching individual targets | 6 | 4% |
| **TOTAL** | **156** | **100%** |

## 3.2. Correlation test

Table 3.14 shows the results from Pearson's correlation test.

The results can be discussed starting with participants' age, which is found to be correlated positively with the job qualification as a manager (0.195 with $p < .05$), with the perceived priority of the PA in respecting the rules (0.228 with $p < .01$), with the horizontal specialization degree (0.351 with $p < .01$), with the vertical specialization degree (0.162 with $p < .05$)

and with the democratic managerial style (0.192 with $p < .05$). Indeed, age has a negative correlation with the job qualification as an officer (– 0.228 with $p < .01$), with the perceived priority of the PA in satisfying public stakeholders (– 0.368 with $p < .01$), with the coercive managerial style (– 0.245 with $p < .01$) and with monetary incentives to improve motivation (– 0.166 with $p < .05$).

**Table 3.14.** Results from Pearson's correlation test.

| | 1 | 2 | 3 | 4 | 5 | 6 | 7 | 8 | 9 | 10 | 11 | 12 | 13 | 14 | 15 | 16 | 17 | 18 | 19 | 20 | 21 | 22 | 23 | 24 | 25 | 26 | 27 | 28 |
|---|---|---|---|---|---|---|---|---|---|---|---|---|---|---|---|---|---|---|---|---|---|---|---|---|---|---|---|---|
| 1. age | 1 | | | | | | | | | | | | | | | | | | | | | | | | | | | |
| 2. PA_central_gov | 0,011 | 1 | | | | | | | | | | | | | | | | | | | | | | | | | | |
| 3. PA_local_gov | 0,054 | -,584** | 1 | | | | | | | | | | | | | | | | | | | | | | | | | |
| 4. PA_health | -0,074 | -0,15 | -,238** | 1 | | | | | | | | | | | | | | | | | | | | | | | | |
| 5. PA_education | -0,008 | -,219** | -,348** | -0,089 | 1 | | | | | | | | | | | | | | | | | | | | | | | |
| 6. PA_research institute | -0,074 | -0,15 | -,238** | -0,061 | -0,089 | 1 | | | | | | | | | | | | | | | | | | | | | | |
| 7. PA_social insurance_institute | 0,036 | -0,085 | -0,135 | -0,035 | 0,051 | -0,035 | 1 | | | | | | | | | | | | | | | | | | | | | |
| 8. role_manager | ,195* | -,239** | 0,072 | -0,098 | 0,034 | 0,144 | ,355** | 1 | | | | | | | | | | | | | | | | | | | | |
| 9. role_officer | -,228** | 0,017 | 0,004 | ,220** | -0,042 | -0,112 | -,157* | -,443** | 1 | | | | | | | | | | | | | | | | | | | |
| 10. role_employee | 0,101 | ,159* | -0,058 | -,165* | 0,02 | 0,014 | -0,093 | -,263** | -,749** | 1 | | | | | | | | | | | | | | | | | | |
| 11. years_service | ,482** | ,328** | -,222** | -,255** | -0,011 | 0,042 | 0,136 | 0,044 | -0,12 | 0,096 | 1 | | | | | | | | | | | | | | | | | |
| 12. PA_priority_rules | ,228** | -0,075 | ,197* | -0,15 | -0,084 | 0,036 | -0,085 | 0,142 | 0,017 | -0,123 | 0,12 | 1 | | | | | | | | | | | | | | | | |
| 13. PA_priority performance | 0,117 | ,295** | -,237** | 0,105 | -0,006 | -0,113 | -0,064 | -,180* | 0,1 | 0,025 | 0,016 | ,278** | 1 | | | | | | | | | | | | | | | |
| 14. PA_priority satisfaction | -,368** | 0,015 | 0,144 | ,210** | -0,098 | -0,055 | 0,011 | -,156 | 0,011 | 0,103 | -,362** | -,239** | -,180* | 1 | | | | | | | | | | | | | | |
| 15. PA_priority_all | -0,04 | -,169* | 0,111 | -0,045 | -0,066 | 0,122 | ,164* | 0,118 | -0,099 | 0,019 | 0,129 | -,520** | -,392** | -,338** | 1 | | | | | | | | | | | | | |
| 16. H_specialization degree | ,351** | 0,065 | ,191* | -,358** | 0,008 | 0,078 | -0,038 | 0,092 | -0,031 | -0,034 | ,344** | ,217** | -0,034 | -,206** | -0,026 | 1 | | | | | | | | | | | | |
| 17. V_specialization degree | ,162* | -,323** | ,173* | -0,099 | ,196* | 0,057 | ,208** | ,267** | -0,083 | -0,109 | 0,082 | 0,078 | -0,086 | 0,055 | 0,099 | ,402** | 1 | | | | | | | | | | | |
| 18. formalization degree | 0,000 | ,166* | -0,129 | 0,039 | -0,115 | 0,039 | 0,067 | -0,027 | 0,092 | -0,08 | -0,022 | -,207** | 0,121 | 0,081 | 0,037 | 0,097 | -0,086 | 1 | | | | | | | | | | |
| 19. managerial style_participative | 0,155 | 0,023 | -0,063 | -0,15 | 0,052 | 0,036 | ,231** | -0,112 | -,158* | ,253** | ,172* | ,218** | -0,048 | -,239** | 0,007 | ,217** | 0,003 | ,207** | 1 | | | | | | | | | |
| 20. managerial style_democratic | ,192* | -0,051 | 0,078 | ,199* | -0,118 | -0,081 | -0,046 | -0,129 | ,159* | 0,076 | ,160* | -,198* | 0,023 | 0,129 | ,249** | -0,088 | 0,116 | 0,093 | -,198* | 1 | | | | | | | | |
| 21. managerial style_coercive | -,245** | 0,065 | 0,109 | 0,014 | -0,11 | ,165* | -0,093 | -0,019 | ,174* | -,174* | -0,154 | -,405** | ,246** | -0,019 | ,188** | -0,107 | -,265** | ,199* | ,405** | -,217** | 1 | | | | | | | |

*see next page*

| Variable | 1 | 2 | 3 | 4 | 5 | 6 | 7 | 8 | 9 | 10 | 11 | 12 | 13 | 14 | 15 | 16 | 17 | 18 | 19 | 20 | 21 | 22 | 23 | 24 | 25 | 26 | 27 | 28 |
|---|---|---|---|---|---|---|---|---|---|---|---|---|---|---|---|---|---|---|---|---|---|---|---|---|---|---|---|---|
| 22. managerial style_anarchy | -0,026 | -0,053 | -0,096 | 0,003 | 0,133 | ,179* | -0,098 | ,206* | 0,122 | -0,02 | 0,112 | ,316** | -,210** | ,326** | ,348** | -0,044 | ,186* | ,450** | -,423** | -,227** | -,465** | 1 | | | | | | |
| 23. personal motivation | -0,035 | 0,075 | -,237** | -0,114 | 0,139 | ,165* | ,212** | 0,12 | 0,037 | -0,049 | 0,056 | 0,038 | 0,047 | 0,071 | -0,022 | ,353** | ,327** | ,163* | 0,148 | ,169* | 0,119 | 0,083 | 1 | | | | | |
| 24. motivation_career | -0,04 | -0,081 | 0,123 | ,289** | 0,056 | 0,122 | -0,12 | 0,004 | -0,099 | 0,104 | 0,104 | 0,095 | 0,123 | 0,118 | -,261** | -0,095 | -0,121 | -0,074 | 0,007 | -0,015 | -0,149 | 0,15 | -0,022 | 1 | | | | |
| 25. motivation_monetary_incentives | -,166* | ,313** | -0,133 | -0,071 | -0,104 | -0,071 | -0,04 | -0,114 | 0,112 | -0,036 | 0,107 | -0,013 | 0,059 | -0,114 | 0,045 | -0,078 | -0,115 | 0,000 | 0,15 | -0,094 | 0,12 | -,201* | 0,131 | -,247** | 1 | | | |
| 26. motivation_non_monetary_incentives | 0,11 | -0,053 | 0,15 | -,172* | 0,133 | -,172* | -0,098 | -0,155 | 0,125 | -0,02 | 0,134 | 0,039 | 0,006 | -0,035 | -0,016 | 0,1 | ,263** | -0,098 | -0,053 | 0,051 | -0,02 | 0,039 | ,187* | -,597** | -,201* | 1 | | |
| 27. motivation_informal_leadership | 0,02 | -0,018 | 0,016 | 0,106 | -0,154 | 0,123 | ,328** | ,300** | -0,05 | ,169* | -0,098 | -,259** | -,195* | -0,012 | ,390** | 0,072 | -0,069 | ,305** | -0,018 | 0,042 | ,178* | 0,039 | -,166* | -,365** | -,123 | -,297** | 1 | |
| 28. conflict degree | -0,119 | -0,027 | 0,036 | 0,112 | 0,077 | -0,077 | -0,043 | 0,087 | 0,084 | -0,155 | -0,043 | -0,027 | -0,079 | -0,052 | 0,121 | -0,084 | 0,146 | -0,034 | -,242** | -0,02 | 0,103 | 0,14 | -0,136 | 0,024 | ,179* | 0,114 | 0,132 | 1 |

*   Correlation is significant at the 0.05 level (2-tailed).
**  Correlation is significant at the 0.01 level (2-tailed).

Relative to the PA of affiliation, the *central government* is positively correlated with the job qualification as an employee (0.159 with p < .05), with the years in service (0.328 with p < .01), with performance as the PA priority (0.295 with p < .01), with the formalization degree (0.166 with p < .05) and with monetary incentives to improve motivation (0.313 with p < .01). A negative correlation exists with the job qualification as a manager (– 0.239 with p < .01) and with the vertical specialization degree (– 0.323 with p < .01).

*Local government* is positively correlated with respecting the rules as the priority (0.197 with p < .05) and with the horizontal (0.191 with p < .05) and vertical (0.173 with p < .05) specialization degrees. It is negatively correlated with the years in service (– 0.222 with p < .01), performance as the priority (– 0.237 with p < .01) and personal motivation (– 0.237 with p < .01). No significant correlations emerge with solutions to improve employees' motivation, with the exception of non-monetary incentives (0.150 by extending p < .10).

*Health and social care* institutions are positively correlated with the job qualification as an officer (0.220 with p < .01), with the democratic managerial style (0.199 with p < .05) and with career development as the motivation incentive (0.289 with p < .01). Negative correlations exist with the years in service (– 0.255 with p.01), with the horizontal specialization degree (– 0.358 with p < .01) and with non-monetary incentives (– 0.172 with p < .05). No significant correlations emerge with the PA priority, with the exception of the satisfaction of stakeholders (0.144 by extending p < .10).

*Education* institutions present only positive correlations with the satisfaction of stakeholders as the priority (0.210 with p < .01) and with the vertical specialization degree (0.196 with p < .05). No significant correlations emerge with the managerial style, with the exception of anarchy (0.133 by extending p < .10). By extending the significance to p < .10, another positive correlation emerges with personal motivation (0.139).

*Research institutes* are positively correlated with an anarchic managerial style (0.179 with p < .05) and with personal motivation (0.165 with p < .05). A negative correlation exists with the coercive managerial style (– 0.165 with p < .05) and with non-monetary incentives (– 0.172 with p <.05). No significant correlations emerge with the PA priority.

*Social insurance institutes* are positively correlated with the job qualification as a manager (0.355 with p < .01), with the vertical specialization degree (0.208 with p < .01), with the participative managerial style (0.231 with p < .01), with personal motivation (0.212 with p < .01) and with the development of informal leadership as a solution to improve motivation (0.328 with p < .01). A negative correlation exists with the job qualification as an officer (– 0.157 with p < .05). No significative correlations emerge with the PA priority.

Regarding the *years in service*, the correlation test also shows a positive correlation with the horizontal specialization degree (0.344 with p < .01) and with the participative (0.172 with p < .05) and democratic (0.160 with p < .05) managerial styles.

Relative to the *managerial styles*, interesting results emerge showing a positive correlation between the participative style and rules as the PA priority (0.218 with p < .01) and between the coercive style and performance as the priority (0.246 with p < .01). Indeed, anarchy surprisingly has a positive correlation with respecting the rules (0.316 with p < .01) and with satisfying public stakeholders (0.326 with p < .01); a negative correlation exists with performance as the priority (– 0.210 with p < .01).

Concerning personal motivation and solutions to improve motivation, other interesting results emerge from the positive correlation between non-monetary incentives and the vertical specialization degree (0.263 with p < .01) and from the positive correlation between the development of informal leadership with the formalization degree (0.305 with p < .01) and with the coercive managerial style (0.178 with p < .05).

## 3.3. Linear regression

Linear regression aims to test the dependence of personal motivation on the main variables characterizing the job assigned and the organizational climate, such as the horizontal and vertical specialization degrees, formalization degree, conflict degree, and managerial style.

Table 3.15 shows the results from the test, with F = 8.507 and sig. = .000.

**Table 3.15.** Results from the regression.

| Coefficients (a) | | | | | |
|---|---|---|---|---|---|
| | Unstandardized Coefficients | | Standardized Coefficients | | |
| Model | B | Std Error | Beta | t | Sig. |
| 1  (Constant) | 0.190 | 0.713 | | 0.267 | 0.790 |
| H specialization degree | 0.467 | 0.169 | 0.224 | 2.764 | 0.006 |
| V specialization degree | 0.612 | 0.180 | 0.275 | 3.391 | 0.001 |
| Formalization degree | 0.220 | 0.088 | 0.195 | 2.500 | 0.014 |
| Conflict degree | -0.257 | 0.111 | -0.175 | -2.310 | 0.022 |
| Managerial style | -0.099 | 0.080 | -0.100 | -1.243 | 0.216 |
| a. Dependent variable: personal motivation | | | | | |
| F = 8.507*** | | | | | |
| Adjusted $R^2$ = 0.195 | | | | | |

With the exception of the managerial style (0.216), all the other variables resulted as significant in the model.

## 3.4. Answers to the research hypotheses

This subsection aims to give more clarity to the answers to the research hypotheses. The first hypothesis was:

*H1: Italian public administrations are still rooted in a bureaucratic model.*

According to Mintzberg (1979), the bureaucratic model is characterized by high standardization, high formalization and centralized decisions. The aim of this model is to achieve internal efficiency by respecting the rules. The following table reports the values of the mentioned characteristics within the analyzed case of Italian public administrations.

**Table 3.16.** Information regarding the answer to H1.

| Variable | Value | Source |
|---|---|---|
| Horizontal specialization degree (from 1 to 4) | 3.15 | Average score on N=156 |
| Vertical specialization degree (from 1 to 4) | 3.21 | Average score on N=156 |
| Formalization degree (from 0 to 5) | 2.50 | Average score on N=156 |
| Respecting the rules and improving performance | 85% | Cumulated percentage of answers "rules" and "performance" |

The values that emerge from the case study highlight that jobs are characterized by both high horizontal and high vertical specialization (3.15 and 3.21 on the 4-point scale from 1 to 4), in line with the settings of the bureaucratic model. Indeed, the formalization degree is well distributed around the average value (2.50 on the 6-point scale from 0 to 5), thus revealing a lower value than that stated by Mintzberg. Relative to the last aspect, achieving internal efficiency, it is possible to note that, by cumulating the percentages resulting from the answers on the PA priorities "rules" and "performance," a very high value emerges (85%).

On the basis of these results, and considering that the formalization degree is nevertheless quite high, it is possible to assert that

H1 is verified.

The second hypothesis was:

*H2a: Jobs' characteristics present high standardization (both horizontal*

*and vertical), high formalization, and high motivation*

and

*H2b: Personal motivation depends positively on a high specialization degree (both horizontal and vertical), high formalization degree, the managerial style, and negatively on a high conflict degree*

As already highlighted in Table 3.16, the averages of both horizontal and vertical specialization degrees are very high (3.15 and 3.21 on the 4-point scale from 1 to 4). Indeed, the formalization degree is perfectly collocated in the middle of the scale (2.50 on the 6-point scale from 0 to 5) and personal motivation is relatively high (3.21 on the 6-point scale from 0 to 5).

Following Mintzberg's (1979) settings of the job specialization matrix, Figure 3.1 shows the application of the matrix to the specific case study, reporting the corresponding number of participants in each square.

**Figure 3.1.** Mintzberg's job specialization matrix.

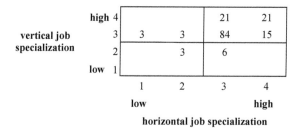

From Figure 3.1 it is easily recognizable that the balance needle is strongly oriented towards highly specialized jobs, typically characterizing the "machine bureaucracy" defined by Mintzberg. Since the high motivation degree also confirms what stated by Merton (1940) on his belief that bureaucrats took pride in their craft, despite the standardized and repetitive tasks, it is possible to assert that

H2a is verified.

The dependence of personal motivation (negatively on a high specialization degree (both horizontal and vertical), high formalization degree and high conflict degree and positively on the managerial style) was tested through a linear regression in which

$$M = \beta_0 + \beta_1 MS + \beta_2 HSd + \beta_3 VSd + \beta_4 Fd - \beta_5 Cd$$

where
M = motivation
MS = managerial style
HSd = horizontal specialization degree
VSd = vertical specialization degree
Fd = formalization degree
Cd = conflict degree

The results from the regression test quite confirm what was hypothesized: a positive relationship emerges with high degrees of specialization (both horizontal and vertical, respectively, with sig. 0.006 and 0.001), a high formalization degree (sig. 0.014). Even the negative impact of the conflict degree is confirmed (sig. 0.022), while no significant relationship emerges with the managerial style (sig. 0.216). Thus,

H2b is partly verified.

The third hypothesis was:

*H3: The managerial styles adopted mainly present the characteristics of a coercive approach.*

Table 3.11 clearly indicates that, of the three managerial styles initially reported within the questionnaire (participative/democratic/coercive), the coercive approach is the most indicated (31%). This result has to be linked to the conflict degree, which on average is 3.25 on the 6-point scale from 0 to 5 and which, by cumulating the percentages of the degrees from 3 to 5, amounts to 87% of cases. Indeed, since 33% of the participants surprisingly indicated anarchy as the most recurring managerial style (or, a better term in this case, organizational model) within their PA of affiliation, it should be asserted that

H3 is not verified.

Even though the third hypothesis is not verified, the result seems to be interesting, since the response "anarchy" represents a possible answer to the question regarding which kind of organizational model is mostly adopted in the Italian setting. The answer is even more interesting considering that it emerged spontaneously from participants' observations.

### 3.5. Focus groups: solutions proposed by the participants

Face-to-face interviews were carried out to gain a better understanding of the participants' opinions about possible interventions in the formalization degree, specialization degree, conflict resolution, desired managerial style, solutions to improve employees' motivation and solutions to overcome bureaucracy's hurdles. Each participant was asked to reply to the questions just after completing the questionnaire, thus providing his/her own suggestions concerning the issues mentioned above. The answers were recorded, transcribed and then labeled for reasons of clarity.

The first question was about interventions in the horizontal job specialization degree (Table 3.17). Most of the participants replied that they had no suggestions regarding this aspect (46%), while 40% answered that there is a need to increase employees' job training. This result is interesting considering the high level of motivation associated with a high level of specialization; this may also be confirmed by the fact that other replies, despite amounting to only 4%, indicated the need to "increase specialization," as the respondents seemed to feel comforted by a high level of specialization.

Other answers did not reach 5%: among these, for instance, the participants reported the need to increase collaboration, the need to increase flexibility and the need for process re-engineering.

**Table 3.17.** Interventions in the horizontal job specialization degree.

| Interventions suggested | N | % |
|---|---|---|
| No suggestion | 72 | 46% |
| Increase flexibility | 6 | 4% |
| Increase specialization | 6 | 4% |
| Increase training | 63 | 40% |
| Increase collaboration | 6 | 4% |
| Process re-engineering | 3 | 2% |
| TOTAL | 156 | 100% |

Even in the case of interventions in the vertical job specialization degree (Table 3.18), most of the participants answered that they had no solutions to suggest (60%). The most important answer related to the vertical specialization degree, "increasing decisional autonomy," only reached 8%. Among the answers that received much more attention, the participants indicated as possible solutions "increasing collaboration" (12%) and "process re-engineering" (10%).

**Table 3.18.** Interventions in the vertical job specialization degree.

| Interventions suggested | N | % |
|---|---|---|
| No suggestion | 93 | 60% |
| Increase decisional autonomy | 12 | 8% |
| Increase collaboration | 18 | 12% |
| Process re-engineering | 15 | 10% |
| Employee involvement | 9 | 6% |
| Simplify norms and procedures | 6 | 4% |
| Improve coordination among activities | 3 | 2% |
| **TOTAL** | **156** | **100%** |

Table 3.19 shows that, with the exception of the high percentage (more than half) of the participants who answered that they did not have solutions to reduce/improve the formalization degree, another high percentage (27%) was achieved by answers related to interventions that involve a clearer attribution of roles and responsibilities, while every other answer only reached 2%.

**Table 3.19.** Interventions in the formalization degree.

| Interventions suggested | N | % |
|---|---|---|
| No | 81 | 52% |
| Monitor the correct application of procedures | 6 | 4% |
| Specific training | 3 | 2% |
| Implement technologies that are useful for sharing | 3 | 2% |
| Increase flexibility | 3 | 2% |
| Increase the culture of work | 3 | 2% |
| Improve communication | 6 | 4% |
| Clearer attribution of roles and responsibilities | 42 | 27% |
| Guarantee transparency | 3 | 2% |
| Reduce the hierarchy | 3 | 2% |
| Increase collaboration | 3 | 2% |
| **TOTAL** | **156** | **100%** |

Concerning the desired managerial style (Table 3.20) within their administration, most of the participants (88%) indicated a participative style, while 10% reported a democratic style and 2% asserted that "leadership is not required; only coercion and authority are needed.".

**Table 3.20.** Desired managerial styles.

| Interventions suggested | N | % |
|---|---|---|
| Coercive | 3 | 2% |
| Participative | 138 | 88% |
| Democratic | 15 | 10% |
| **TOTAL** | **156** | **100%** |

Table 3.21 shows the answers related to the interventions for conflict resolution. Half of the participants indicated "sharing targets with employees," and 19% indicated "creating a positive organizational climate.".

**Table 3.21.** Conflict resolution.

| Interventions suggested | N | % |
|---|---|---|
| Sharing targets with employees | 78 | 50% |
| Managing HR with incentives | 27 | 17% |
| Creating a positive organizational climate | 30 | 19% |
| Creating a uniform culture | 18 | 12% |
| Distributive justice | 3 | 2% |
| **TOTAL** | **156** | **100%** |

Table 3.22 reports the solutions proposed by the participants to improve employees' motivation. The results show a strong preference for career development possibilities (42%) and monetary incentives (33%), while scarce attention is devoted to other kinds of solutions, such as non-monetary incentives (8%), developing informal and participative leadership (15%) and using superiors' behaviors as an example for employees' behaviors (2%).

**Table 3.22.** Solutions to improve motivation.

| Interventions suggested | N | % |
|---|---|---|
| Monetary incentives | 51 | 33% |
| Career development | 66 | 42% |
| Non-monetary incentives | 12 | 8% |
| Developing informal and participative leadership | 24 | 15% |
| Superiors adopting behaviors to be used as an example for employees | 3 | 2% |
| **TOTAL** | **156** | **100%** |

The following table shows the results of the discussion with the participants about the solutions that they would propose to resolve bureaucracy's
inefficiencies. Interestingly, 62% of the participants gave answers that can
be labeled as "working on individual behaviors," while 29% proposed to
adopt organizational models based on project management. Among the
other answers, it is worth highlighting that some participants (4%) reported the need to reduce the excessive regulations.

**Table 3.23.** Solutions for overcoming bureaucracy's inefficiencies.

| Interventions suggested | N | % |
|---|---|---|
| Working on individual behaviors | 96 | 62% |
| Managing by projects | 45 | 29% |
| Building a culture of service | 3 | 2% |
| Seeking efficiency | 3 | 2% |
| Increasing reunions | 3 | 2% |
| Reducing the excessive regulations | 6 | 4% |
| TOTAL | 156 | 100% |

## 4. Discussion

The discussion of the results will follow two main directions, aiming to
highlight the most recurring models by type of public administration and
the overall model recurring in the Italian public sector.

Interestingly, by examining the characteristics of the central government
emerging from the analysis, the resulting model reflect perfectly the New
Public Management (NPM) features. In fact, there is a great focus on performance confirmed by a perfect correlation (0.295 with $p = .000$) between
central government and performance as the priority. Additionally, there are
positive correlations with the high formalization degree (0.166 with $p <$
$.05$) and developed role for employees (0.159 with $p < .05$), in line with the
decentralization principle led by the NPM approach. Finally, there is also a
positive correlation with monetary incentives (0.313 with $p = .000$), again in
line with the NPM principle according to which employees are much more
motivated by monetary incentives.

As the opposite of this model, there is the model recurring in local government, mostly presenting the characteristics of classical bureaucracy. In
this case the priority is represented by the attention to rules (0.197 with $p <$
$.05$), and there is a positive correlation with the horizontal (0.191 with $p <$
$.05$) and the vertical (0.173 with $p < .05$) specialization degree, while a negative correlation exists with performance ($- 0.222$ with $p < .01$). Along with

this a negative correlation with motivation exists (− 0.237 with p < .01), thus confirming the low motivation degree associated with the bureaucratic model.

This result might be highlighted considering that local governments are characterized by highly standardized and repetitive tasks oriented towards providing basic services to the citizenship. This, on one side, assures the possibility to reply quite quickly to similar requests, but, on the other side, due to the proximity of these institutions to the citizenship, it might also create problems when variations to a standardized service are requested. This represents an important issue to be debated, especially in consideration of the increasing degree of complexity that characterizes the modern society and leads to the need to find customized solutions for citizens/customers/stakeholders.

Health and social care institutions confirm the adoption of the professional bureaucracy model by showing a positive correlation with the orientation towards customer satisfaction (0.144 extending p < .10) and with career development as the main incentive to improve employees' motivation (0.289 with p = .000).

Public administrations in the education and research fields show positive correlations with the characteristics concerning anarchy, even though they also show a strong and positive correlation with high degrees of motivation. This could be highlighted in association with the fact that Italian institutions in these fields suffer from the assignment of low budgets to their activities; thus, employees working in these institutions require high degrees of intrinsic motivation to carry out their activities and develop a way of working and reasoning that might help them to overcome the highly formal and staid bureaucratic procedures, thus resulting in a sort of anarchy.

Social insurance institutions proved to be the most informal type of public administration due to the positive correlation with the adoption of a participative managerial style (0.231 with p < .01), a high motivation degree (0.212 with p < .01) and a motivation incentive represented by the presence of informal leadership (0.328 with p = .000). This result is, at least, surprising, since it is expected that this kind of public administration is strongly characterized by bureaucratic features.

Finally, to verify which model occurs overall in the Italian public sector, Mintzberg's (1979) specialization matrix was applied to determine whether Weber's statement about the high specialization degree associated with the bureaucratic model also occurs in the specific case analyzed. On this basis tasks' characteristics, as they emerged from the participants' answers about their tasks' specialization degrees, were analyzed. The results from the analysis show high degrees of specialization (both horizontal and vertical), thus confirming that the tasks performed by the participants may be collocated perfectly within the bureaucratic domain.

According to the literature, these kinds of tasks are always associated with a low motivation degree due to the high specialization and repetition of the activities carried out by employees. Indeed, here it has been considered what stated by Merton (1940) on the fact that bureaucrats took pride in their craft, which leads them to resist changes in established routines. The results from the analysis are perfectly in line with this claim, showing a high degree of motivation associated to high degrees of horizontal and vertical specialization. The results from the analysis indeed show that participants have a quite high motivation degree (3.21 on a scale from 0 to 5).

On this ground, it could be argued that Italian public employees are "happy bureaucrats": they are strongly motivated by performing highly standardized tasks with low responsibilities, by the presence of monetary incentives (33%), and by having career development possibilities (42%).

Along with these results, another interesting discussion emerges considering the conflict degree: by cumulating the percentages associated with the higher degrees (3, 4 and 5), an overall percentage of 87% emerged, indicating a very high degree of conflict occurring within the observed public administrations. These data, associated with the desire expressed by 88% of the participants for a different managerial/leadership style that is much more oriented towards a participative one, produce an issue related to the low degree of involvement of employees in the processes and a low sharing climate. This is also confirmed by the answers given by the participants about conflict resolution, in which 50% indicated the need for shared targets and 19% reported the need to create a positive organizational climate.

Again, the fact that, in reporting which kind of style/organizational model is adopted within their administrations, 33% of the participants indicated "anarchy" shows that Italian public administrations are often characterized by the absence of a well-structured organizational model, with no clear attribution of roles and responsibilities, as highlighted by 27% of the participants when asked which kind of interventions they imagined in the formalization degree.

## 5. Final remarks and research limits

To conclude this analysis, it is worth highlighting that two faces of the Italian public sector emerged: on one side, there are "happy bureaucrats," surprisingly strongly motivated by repetitive and standardized tasks and monetary incentives and strongly convinced to maintain the *status quo*, as revealed by the high percentages of participants not reporting/proposing solutions to solve problems related to the specialization and formalization degrees.

A consideration related to this result might be the fact that the introduction of NPM principles has probably only led to employees' target transposition from rules to the achievement of personal targets related to monetary incentives.

On the other side, there are employees working in contexts in which anarchy is the most recurring organizational model, with no clear attribution of roles and responsibilities and no employee involvement.

Considering the results produced by this analysis, it seems that in Italy the reform led by the NPM principles during the 1990s has never been completed. The NPM principles have only been applied partially to some aspects of the public service provision process, while it appears that managers and employees are still rooted in the ancient bureaucratic way of thinking, operating and behaving. Moreover, they appear to be "happy" to be bureaucrats, despite being entrapped in standardized and repetitive tasks. It appears that the NPM introduction of monetary incentives, related to the achievement of specific targets, is a sufficient reward and motivating factors for Italian public servants.

On this basis, the results from this analysis show that a decoupling is taking place between theory and practice. In fact, while the theory suggests that employees carrying out repetitive tasks suffer from turnover, alienation, and low motivation, in practice, at least in the case analyzed, employees show a high degree of motivation, as it seems that they are defending the *status quo* that allows "doing less for having more," as stated by Merton (1940) in contending that bureaucrats took pride in their craft and resist to changes in their working routines.

Surely, an action that the Italian Government should consider taking is related to a tentative to reduce the excessive regulations, which often create overlapping laws and confusing situations, for which public employees themselves have no instruments to find solutions.

Then, the fact that many of the participants spontaneously indicated "anarchy" as the "organizational model" operating in their administration, shows that the Italian Government needs to rethink the way in which public administrations are organized and managed, especially in consideration of the fact that 27% of the participants highlighted no clear attribution of roles and responsibilities within their administrations.

Thus, the results obtained from the questionnaires and interviews confirm that the core problem to be faced within public administrations is related to the lack of an organizational culture oriented towards managing the public in the public interest and not in the interest of managers and employees trying to attain personal performance rewards. The second step, strictly related to this, is the recourse to a behavioral approach, as shown in the second chapter of this book, to assure that managers' and employees' behaviors are in line with the development of a different culture that should then improve the way in which public administrations are managed and organized to pursue the public interest.

A limitation of the analysis conducted in this chapter can be found in the fact that the Italian setting may represent a very narrow focus and that, due to its peculiar characteristics and conditions, results from this setting might be difficult to replicate or expand to other settings. At the same time, it should be recognized that the case analyzed contributes in giving insights in one of countries belonging to the group of Continental European countries - especially those in the Southern area - less regarded and still under-investigated by the literature, despite their peculiarities.

## 6. References

Ahn M.J., and Bretschneider S. (2011), Politics of E-Government: E-Government and the Political Control of Bureaucracy, *Public Administration Review*, vol. 71, no. 3, pp. 414-424. doi: 10.1111/j.1540-6210.2011.02225.x.

Alexander D., Lewis J.M., and Considine M. (2011), How Politicians and Bureaucrats Network: A Comparison Across Governments, *Public Administration*, vol. 89, no. 4, pp. 1274-1292. doi: 10.1111/j.1467-9299.2010.01890.x.

Bang H.P. (2004), Culture Governance: Governing Self-Reflexive Modernity, *Public Administration*, vol. 82, no. 1, pp. 157-190, doi: 10.1111/j.0033-3298.2004.00389.x.

Berg A.M. (2006), Transforming public services – transforming the public servant?, *International Journal of Public Sector Management*, vol. 19, no. 6, pp. 556-568, doi: 10.1108/09513550610686627.

Bode I., and Dent M. (2014), Converging hybrid worlds? Medicine and hospital management in Europe, *International Journal of Public Sector Management*, vol. 27, no. 5, doi: 10.1108/IJPSM-01-2013-0011.

Callanan M. (2005), Institutionalizing Participation and Governance? New Participative Structures in Local Government in Ireland, *Public Administration*, vol. 83, no. 4, pp. 909-929. doi: 10.1111/j.0033-3298.2005.00483.x.

Carey G., and Matthews M. (2017), Methods for Delivering Complex Social Services: Exploring adaptive management and regulation in the Australian national disability insurance scheme, *Public Management Review*, vol. 19, no. 2, pp. 194-211, doi:10.1080/14719037.2016.1148194.

Charlesworth J., Clarke J., and Cochrane A. (1996), Tangled Webs? Managing Local Mixed Economies Of Care, *Public Administration*, vol. 74, no. 1, pp. 67-88, doi: 10.1111/j.1467-9299.1996.tb00858.x.

Cloutier C., Denis J.L., Langley A., and Lamothe L. (2016), Agency at the Managerial Interface: Public Sector Reform as Institutional Work, *Journal of Public Administration Research and Theory*, vol. 26, no. 2, pp. 259-276, doi: 10.1093/jopart/muv009.

Considine M. (2000), Contract Regimes and Reflexive Governance: Comparing Employment Service Reforms in the United Kingdom, the Netherlands, New Zealand and Australia, *Public Administration*, vol. 78, no. 3, pp. 613-638, doi: 10.1111/1467-9299.00221.

Correia, T., and Denis, J.L. (2016), Hybrid management, organizational configuration, and medical professionalism: evidence from the establishment of a clinical directorate in Portugal, *BMC Health Services Research*, vol. 16, SI 2, pp. 161, doi: 10.1186/s12913-016-1398-2.

Currie G., Grubnic S., and Hodges R. (2011), Leadership In Public Services Networks: Antecedents, Process And Outcome, *Public Administration*, vol. 89, no. 2, pp. 242-264, doi: 10.1111/J.1467-9299.2011.01931.X.

Currie, G., and Procter, S.J. (2005), The antecedents of middle managers' strategic contribution: The case of a professional bureaucracy, *Journal Of Management Studies*, vol. 42, no. 7, pp. 1325-1356, doi: 10.1111/j.1467-6486.2005.00546.x.

De Boer H.F., Enders J., and Leisyte L. (2007), Public Sector Reform In Dutch Higher Education: The Organizational Transformation Of The University, *Public Administration*, vol. 85, no. 1, pp. 27-46, doi: 10.1111/j.1467-9299.2007.00632.x.

Entwistle T., and Martin S. (2005), From Competition to Collaboration in Public Service Delivery: A New Agenda for Research, *Public Administration*, vol. 83, no. 1, pp. 233-242, doi: 10.1111/j.0033-3298.2005.00446.x.

Finn, R., Currie, G., and Martin G. (2010), Team Work in Context: Institutional Mediation in the Public-service Professional Bureaucracy, *Organization Studies*, vol. 31, no. 8, pp. 1069-1097, doi: 10.1177/0170840610376142.

Fotaki M. (2011), Towards Developing New Partnerships In Public Services: Users As Consumers, Citizens And/Or Co-Producers In Health And Social Care In England And Sweden, *Public Administration*, vol. 89, no. 3, pp. 933-955, doi: 10.1111/j.1467-9299.2010.01879.x.

Gatenby M., Rees C., Truss C., Alfes K., and Soane E. (2015), Managing Change, or Changing Managers? The role of middle managers in UK public service reform, *Public Management Review*, vol. 17, no. 8, pp. 1124-1145, doi: 10.1080/14719037.2014.895028.

Geddes L., (2012), In Search of Collaborative Public Management, *Public Management Review*, vol. 14, no. 7, pp. 947-966, doi: 10.1080/14719037.2011.650057.

Germov, J. (2005), Managerialism in the Australian public health sector: towards the hyper-rationalisation of professional bureaucracies, *Sociology Of Health & Illness*, vol. 27, no. 6, pp. 738-758, doi: 10.1111/j.1467-9566.2005.00472.x.

Gourdin, G., and Schepers, R. (2009), Hospital governance and the medical practitioner in Belgium, *Journal Of Health Organization And Management*, vol. 23, no. 3, pp. 319-331, doi: 10.1108/14777260910966744.

Hammerschmid G., and Meyer R.E. (2005), New Public Management in Austria: Local Variation on a Global Theme?, *Public Administration*, vol. 83, no. 3, pp. 709-733, doi: 10.1111/j.0033-3298.2005.00471.x.

Jeffares S., and Skelcher C. (2011), Democratic Subjectivities In Network Governance: A Q Methodology Study Of English And Dutch Public Managers, *Public Administration*, vol. 89, no. 4, pp. 1253-1273, doi: 10.1111/j.1467-9299.2010.01888.x.

Kane J., and Patapan H. (2006), In Search of Prudence: The Hidden Problem of Managerial Reform, *Public Administration Review*, vol. 66, no. 5, pp. 711-724, doi: 10.1111/j.1540-6210.2006.00636.x.

Kelly J. (2006), Central Regulation Of English Local Authorities: An Example Of Meta-Governance?, *Public Administration*, vol. 84, no. 3, pp. 603-621, doi: 10.1111/j.1467-9299.2006.00604.x.

Kickert W.J.M. (2005), Distinctiveness in the study of public management in Europe, *Public Management Review*, vol. 7, no. 4, pp. 537-563, doi: 10.1080/14719030500362470.

Kickert W.J.M. (2011), Distinctiveness Of Administrative Reform In Greece, Italy, Portugal And Spain. Common Characteristics Of Context, Administrations And Reforms, *Public Administration*, vol. 89, no. 3, pp. 801-818, doi: 10.1111/j.1467-9299.2010.01862.x.

Kinder T. (2012), Learning, Innovating and Performance in Post-New Public Management of Locally Delivered Public Services, *Public Management Review*, vol. 14, no. 3, pp. 403-428, doi: 10.1080/14719037.2011.637408.

Kirkpatrick I. (1999), Managers or Colleagues?, *Public Management: An International Journal of Research and Theory*, vol. 1, no. 4, pp. 489-509, doi: 10.1080/14719039900000023.

Kirkpatrick I., and Ackroyd S. (2003), Transforming the professional archetype?, *Public Management Review*, vol. 5, no. 4, pp. 509-529. doi: 10.1080/1471903032000178563.

Kitchener M., and Gask L. (2003), NPM merger mania. Lessons from an early case, *Public Management Review*, vol. 5, no. 1, pp. 19-44. doi: 10.1080/1461667022000028843.

Knott J.H., Miller G.J. (2006), Social welfare, corruption and credibility, *Public Management Review*, vol. 8, no. 2, pp. 227-252, doi: 10.1080/14719030600587455.

Knott J.H. (2011), Federalist No. 10: Are Factions the Problem in Creating Democratic Accountability in the Public Interest?, *Public Administration Review*, vol. 71, SI 1, pp. s29-s36, doi: 10.1111/j.1540-6210.2011.02459.x.

Kooiman J., Jentoft S. (2009), Meta-governance: values, norms and principles, and the making of hard choices, *Public Administration*, vol. 87, no. 4, pp. 818-836. doi: 10.1111/j.1467-9299.2009.01780.x.

Kothari S., and Handscombe, R.D. (2007), Sweep or seep? Structure, culture, enterprise and universities, *Management Decision*, vol. 45, no. 1, pp. 43-61, doi: 10.1108/00251740710718953.

Learmonth M. (2005), Doing Things with Words: The Case of 'Management' and 'Administration', *Public Administration*, vol. 83, no. 3, pp. 617-637, doi: 10.1111/j.0033-3298.2005.00465.x.

Lega, F., and DePietro, C. (2005), Converging patterns in hospital organization: beyond the professional bureaucracy, *Health Policy*, vol. 74, no. 3, pp. 261-281, doi: 10.1016/j.healthpol.2005.01.010.

Lehmann Nielsen V. (2006), Are Street-Level Bureaucrats Compelled Or Enticed To Cope?, *Public Administration*, vol. 84, no. 4, pp. 861-889, doi: 10.1111/j.1467-9299.2006.00616.x.

Magone J.M. (2011), The Difficult Transformation Of State And Public Administration In Portugal. Europeanization And The Persistence Of Neo-Patrimonialism, *Public Administration*, vol. 89, no. 3, pp. 756-782, doi: 10.1111/j.1467-9299.2011.01913.x.

Martin G.P. (2011), The Third Sector, User Involvement And Public Service Reform: A Case Study In The Co-Governance Of Health Service Provision, *Public Administration*, vol. 89, no. 3, pp. 909-932, doi: 10.1111/j.1467-9299.2011.01910.x.

Martin G.P., Currie G., and Finn R. (2009), Leadership, Service Reform, and Public-Service Networks: The Case of Cancer-Genetics Pilots in the English NHS, *Journal of Public Administration Research and Theory*, vol. 19, no. 4, pp. 769-794, doi:10.1093/jopart/mun016.

McGivern G., Currie G., Ferlie E., Fitzgerald L., and Waring J. (2015), Hybrid Manager-Professionals' Identity Work: The Maintenance And Hybridization Of Medical Professionalism In Managerial Contexts, *Public Administration*, vol. 93, no. 2, pp. 412-432, doi: 10.1111/padm.12119.

Meier K.J., and Bohte J. (2001), Structure and Discretion: Missing Links in Representative Bureaucracy, *Journal of Public Administration Research and Theory*, vol. 11, no. 4, pp. 455-470, doi: 10.1093/oxfordjournals.jpart.a003511.

Meyer R.E., Egger-Peitler I., Höllerer M.A., Hammerschmid G. (2014), Of Bureaucrats And Passionate Public Managers: Institutional Logics, Executive Identities, And Public Service Motivation, *Public Administration*, vol. 92, no. 4, pp. 861-885, doi: 10.1111/j.1467-9299.2012.02105.x.

Meynhardt T., and Diefenbach F. E. (2012), What Drives Entrepreneurial Orientation in the Public Sector? Evidence from Germany's Federal Labor Agency, *Journal of Public Administration Research and Theory*, vol. 22, no. 4, pp. 761-792, doi:10.1093/jopart/mus013.

Mintzberg, H. (1979), *The Structuring of Organizations*, Englewood Cliffs: Prentice Hall.

Noordegraaf M., and Abma T. (2003), Management by Measurement? Public Management Practices Amidst Ambiguity, *Public Administration*, vol. 81, no. 4, pp. 853-871, doi: 10.1111/j.0033-3298.2003.00374.x.

Noordegraaf M., and De Wit B. (2012), Responses To Managerialism: How Management Pressures Affect Managerial Relations And Loyalties In Education, *Public Administration*, vol. 90, no. 4, pp. 957-973, doi: 10.1111/j.1467-9299.2012.02068.x.

Ongaro E. (2006), The Dynamics Of Devolution Processes In Legalistic Countries: Organizational Change In The Italian Public Sector, *Public Administration*, vol. 84, no. 3, pp. 737-770, doi: 10.1111/j.1467-9299.2006.00610.x.

Orr K., and Vince R. (2009), Traditions Of Local Government, *Public Administration*, vol. 87, no. 3, pp. 655-677, doi: 10.1111/j.1467-9299.2009.01770.x.

Pollitt C. (2009), Bureaucracies Remember, Post-Bureaucratic Organizations Forget?, *Public Administration*, vol. 87, no. 2, pp. 198-218, doi: 10.1111/J.1467-9299.2008.01738.X.

Raadschelders J.C.N. (1995), Rediscovering Citizenship: Historical And Contemporary Reflections, *Public Administration*, vol. 73, no. 4, pp. 611-625. doi: 10.1111/j.1467-9299.1995.tb00849.x.

Rothstein, H., Downer, J. (2012), 'Renewing Defra': Exploring the emergence of risk-based policymaking in UK central government, *Public Administration*, vol. 90, pp. 781-799. doi:10.1111/j.1467-9299.2011.01999.x.

Seibel W. (2010), Beyond Bureaucracy – Public Administration as Political Integrator and Non-Weberian Thought in Germany, *Public Administration Review*, vol. 70, no. 5, pp. 719-730, doi: 10.1111/j.1540-6210.2010.02200.x.

Tichelar, M. (1997), Professional bureaucracy as a barrier to management learning in the public services: A personal reflection, *Local Government Studies*, vol. 23, no. 2, pp. 14-25. doi: 10.1080/03003939708433862.

Vinot D. (2014), Transforming hospital management à la francaise: The new role of clinical managers in French public hospitals, *International Journal of Public Sector Management*, vol. 27 (5): pp. 406-416, doi: 10.1108/IJPSM-06-2012-0067.

Voets J., Verhoest K., and Molenveld A. (2015), Coordinating for Integrated Youth Care: The need for smart metagovernance, *Public Management Review*, vol. 17, no. 7, pp. 981-1001, doi: 10.1080/14719037.2015.1029347.

Williams B.N., Kang S.-C., and Johnson J. (2016), (Co)-Contamination as the Dark Side of Co-Production: Public value failures in co-production processes, *Public Management Review*, vol. 18, no. 5, pp. 692-717, doi: 10.1080/14719037.2015.1111660.

# CONCLUSIONS

This book aimed to provide insights into the complex, and often unclear, context of the public sector, and to describe a new approach to the analysis and management of public organizations.

Public administrations are historically rooted in the bureaucratic model, as described by Weber (1922). Weber described bureaucracy in its pure form as the most efficient and rational way of organizing. According to the author, bureaucratization was the key part of the rational-legal authority and the key process in the ongoing rationalization of Western society. Weber individuated several preconditions for the emergence of bureaucracy: the growth in space and population being administered, the growth in complexity of the administrative tasks being carried out, and the existence of a monetary economy requiring a more efficient administrative system. There was the belief that a system of transparent rules was better than a system without rules. Weber's ideal-typical bureaucracy is characterized by hierarchical organization; delineated lines of authority in a fixed area of activity; high standardized of tasks; action taken on the basis of, and recorded in, written rules; bureaucratic officials needing expert training; rules implemented by neutral officials; career advancement made through competition and based on technical qualifications.

This model encountered several problems as the "local" world started changing toward a more globalized one. In this new context, the public sector has several times demonstrated its incapacity to re-adapt to the modern world. The reasons behind this crisis can be partly found in the highly debated failure of the classic bureaucracy. Thus, over time, the term "bureaucracy" has become synonymous with "inefficiency," given the failure of several of its premises. During the 1940s and 1950s, studies in the literature already advanced some negative aspects emerging from the application of bureaucratic models that are still recognized today. First, under the economic point of view authors contend inefficiency and low performance (Rothstein & Downer, 2012). Second, under the organizational aspect the debate recognizes the low motivation of employees (Meyer et al., 2014) and situations such as turnover, alienation (Tichelar, 1997), lack of human resource policies (Magone, 2011), and lack of flexibility (Considine, 2000). Third, under the social point of view literature sees episodes of corruption (Knott & Miller, 2006), absenteeism, and opportunism (Ahn & Bretschneider, 2011; Considine, 2000; Knott, 2011; Knott & Miller, 2006). Finally, under the institutional lens studies raise issues of the poor quality of public services delivered (Magone, 2011), low attention toward the public interest (Lynn, 2001), and the treating of citizens more as passive users than as active customers (Ahn & Bretschneider, 2011).

These critics become even more relevant if contextualized in a globalized world, and ask for more flexibility. The higher complexity characterizing the modern world requires organizational models and lean procedures able to adapt to a new and ever-changing context.

Searching for responses to bureaucratic inefficiency and putting the accent on the performance and "managerialization" of the public administration became key points of the New Public Management (NPM) (Hood, 1991). In the context of state failure, of poor performance of its bureaucracies, and with its focus on results and on optimizing the public budget, the managerial approach promised improvements in bureaucratic efficiency and accountability following agency theory, through the creation of incentive systems that would direct bureaucrats (the agents) to meet targets set by policy makers, political representatives, and citizens (principals) in the provision of public goods and services.

Significant research after the mid-2000s pointed out a series of unsolved contradictions in the NPM approach, arguing that NPM failed to deliver better value, since proponents underestimate the complexity permeating the public sector (Lapsley, 2008; 2009). An alternative perspective is that new forms of governance were superseding managerialism (Kooiman & Jentoft, 2009). Osborne (2010a; 2010b), in fact, put new public governance (NPG) at the center of a post-NPM debate, based on involving more actors (both public and private), creating more consensus and voluntary participation in decision-making processes, and establishing collaborative relationships and networks. However, according to Noordegraaf and Abma (2003), it should be acknowledged that this approach was weaker than the previous one, because trends such as NPM (Hood, 1991), "performance-oriented management" (Pollitt & Bouckaert, 2000), and the rise of the "audit society" (Power, 1999) indicate that the world of public management has now become, first and foremost, a world of measurement (Noordegraaf & Abma, 2003). Along with this issue, the literature (e.g., Klijn, 2008; Meek, 2010) still acknowledges that public systems are strongly anchored to an ancient tradition of bureaucratic, standardized, and repeated activities characterized by high rationality (Meek, 2010).

On these premises, because many issues remain unsolved, this book aimed at answering the following research questions: *Which organizational features characterize modern public administrations? What factors influence the predominance of different models? What aspects characterize the activities carried out by public servants?*

The book has been structured in three chapters.

The first chapter provided a systematic literature review to answer two fundamental, albeit inconclusively debated questions. The review aimed to detect the limitations and concerns affecting public-sector bureaucracies. Second, it enabled a discussion on the models possibly overcoming extant limitations and improving public-sector organizations and administrations. In finding answers to these questions, a fundamental premise has been related to the issues of bureaucracy and complexity within the public sector, paying particular attention to those factors, both external and internal, that contribute to qualifying public-sector organizations as complex bureaucracies.

The analyzed literature critically reviews all the models/approaches and proposes interesting solutions to be adopted to improve the models. For instance, Kickert (2011) resumes the main criticism of all public administration models. According to the author, bureaucracy is characterized by immobility and inertia, formalism, clientelism, patronage, and corruption; NPM reforms led to very small changes, and with NPG no substantial changes occurred with respect to the NPM approach. Even in terms of solutions, academics provided interesting suggestions, for instance in terms of good managerial practices, flexible models, professionals' autonomy, and engagement of the civil society.

Two main gaps emerge from the analysis of the literature. First, there are no studies analyzing the features of the organizational model and the activities carried out by public servants in modern public administrations, or their behaviors. Attention has always been paid to the rules driving the public administration, following the bureaucratic model; then on the performance, following the NPM reforms; and finally on the search for collaboration, networks, and partnerships in light of the NPG approach. Even if these aspects are key to set up organizational change processes of wide impact, they represent only a part of the more complex issue regarding the public sector. In fact, because organizations are basically made of individuals, and because the main criticisms of bureaucratic models are related to negative individual behaviors such as episodes of corruption, rent-seeking, and opportunism, there has been a strong lack of attention toward individuals and their behaviors. Some academics (e.g., Knott & Miller, 2006) argue that public models led political elites to engage in corruption and extracting rents. Thus, increased levels of transparency, professionalism, and legality should ensure that public managers do not engage in rent extraction. On this ground, in fact, it is worth noting that effective processes of change may only occur when they also involve aspects such as organizational culture and individuals' behaviors.

The second gap is the lack of attention toward the countries of Southern Europe. These countries present interesting and peculiar characteristics due to historical, cultural, and political differences with respect to Anglo-Saxon and other Continental European countries. In fact, by looking at studies of public administration, because nuances in the model do exist, it can be seen that since 1991 the literature has mainly concentrated on Anglo-Saxon countries (Alexander et al., 2011; Callanan, 2005; Carey & Matthews, 2017; Charlesworth et al., 1996; Cloutier et al., 2016; Considine, 2000; Currie & Procter, 2005; Entwistle & Martin, 2005; Finn et al., 2010; Gatenby et al., 2015; Germov, 2005; Kane & Patapan, 2006; Kelly, 2006; Kinder, 2012; Kirkpatrick & Ackroyd, 2003; Kirkpatrick, 1999; Kitchener & Gask, 2003; Knott & Miller, 2006; Knott, 2011; Kothari & Handscombe, 2007; Learmonth, 2005; Martin, 2011; McGivern et al., 2015; Meier & Bohte, 2001; Orr & Vince, 2009; Pollitt, 2009; Rothstein & Downer, 2012; Williams et al., 2016), while less attention has been devoted to the countries of Continental Europe (Bang, 2004; Berg, 2006; Bode & Dent, 2014; Currie et al., 2011; De Boer et al., 2007; Fotaki, 2011; Geddes, 2012; Gourdin & Schepers, 2009; Hammerschmid & Meyer, 2005; Jeffares & Skelcher, 2011; Kickert, 2005; Lega & DePietro, 2005; Nielsen, 2006; Martin et al., 2009; Meyer et al., 2014; Meynhardt & Diefenbach, 2012; Noordegraaf & De Wit, 2012; Raadschelders, 1995; Seibel, 2010; Vinot, 2014; Voets et al., 2015), especially to those in the Southern area (Correia & Denis, 2016; Kickert, 2005, 2011; Lega & DePietro, 2005; Magone, 2011; Ongaro, 2006).

Chapters 2 and 3 aimed to find answers to these gaps. In particular, the book contends that new models for public administrations should be developed by paying much more attention to individual interactions, group dynamics, leadership, and the development of soft skills for public managers, useful to enhance positive individual behaviors and to properly manage people and activities in a highly standardized context.

Chapter 2 emphasized the importance of individual behaviors in the public service environment, because behaviors shape and are shaped by personal qualities, interpersonal relationships, and context-related variables. The effects on dimensions such as leadership, human resource management, and interactions were examined by relating them both to operational management and change management.

This chapter discussed the main features of the behavioral approach, first by assessing the literature in the for-profit sector, and also relying upon the framework provided by Huse (2007), which prompted several studies on the behavioral approach and its importance.

It has been argued that research in the for-profit sector has devoted great attention to the behavioral approach, even if the accent has been mainly put on the board of directors. In this regard, the framework provided by Huse (2007) also analyzed the behaviors within the board of directors, through four main dimensions: board members, interactions, structures and leadership, and decision-making culture. These dimensions enable the understanding of how the board composition, interactions among board members, characteristics of the organizational structure, features of leadership, and organizational climate (in terms of cohesiveness and degree of conflict) influence the board performance and the quality of the board decision-making process.

Despite the reference to the for-profit sector and the board of directors, the framework provided by Huse (2007) shows great potential for generally understanding human behaviors within organization. Thus, tentative work in adapting Huse's framework to the public sector has been done by first assessing specific literature on the behavioral approach in the public domain, using the ISI Web of Knowledge research engine. Results reveal that a major focus has been on aspects concerning the "hard" part of the organization, such as human resources management and structure, culture, and values, while less attention is paid toward "soft" aspects such as individual interactions and organizational climate. Then, building on these results, the framework proposed by Huse (2007) has been adapted by introducing four dimensions to analyze the behaviors within public organizations: human resources management; culture, leadership, and structures; interactions; and organizational climate.

It has been argued that the way in which human resources are managed, in terms of selection, evaluation assessment, motivation, and incentives, has a great impact on employees' behaviors in the public sector, where the peculiar characteristics of the tasks to be carried out may engender alienation and turnover.

In the same way, organizational values/culture and leadership style may positively or negatively affect employees' behaviors. Here reference might also be made to managers/superiors adopting behaviors as an example for employees: improper or unethical behavior by managers can engender negative, imitative behavior by employees.

Interactions are also important in explaining employees' behaviors. Studies find that interaction difficulties often affect individual work performance and jeopardize complete achievement of tasks. Employees' interactions are strongly affected by workplace trust: if people trust each other, willingness to work and interact will increase. Power and influence also may affect individual behavior. On one side, the possibility to exert power and influence over other people represents a motivating factor (McClelland, 1961); on the other side, these actions could negatively affect the behaviors of people who suffer the effects.

The organizational climate represents another key factor determining employees' behaviors. Within any organization a high level of cohesiveness and commitment enables and increases willingness to work with others, while a high degree of conflict engenders negative behaviors and employee departures.

Finally, the last section of this chapter summarized the key features of the behavioral approach, with the aim of explaining how to locate it within studies on the public sector. A review of previous models by Geddes (2012) was a starting point of the discussion. Geddes (2012) analyzed Public Administration, NPM, and Collaborative Public Management through eleven management dimensions: performance, accountability, community engagement, values, leadership, employment relations, management tasks, decision making, structure, processes, and change. Then the author individuated the prevailing model for each management dimension, shown in the first three columns of Table 2.2.

Two more columns in Table 2.2 highlight what might be the contribution of the behavioral approach in improving previous models on public administration. The behavioral approach primarily considers the individual and individual behaviors, because they represent the basis of the organizational analysis. Thus, to effectively solve the problems in organizations and public administrations, an in-depth understanding of the drivers of human behaviors is needed.

In evaluating the eleven management dimensions, employee reactions and behaviors should always be considered. Incentives – both monetary and nonmonetary – and other solutions, such as increasing employees' involvement in the decision-making process, might help in aligning individual behaviors to the public administration targets, but this also needs increased individual accountability related to low performance or missed goals.

The main suggestion deriving from the behavioral approach is that the hierarchy characterizing the bureaucratic approach should be maintained, to guarantee that control over activities is not lost, but at the same time it should involve increased flexibility, to avoid repetitive tasks and related issues. This may only occur if human resource management, culture, and structures are oriented towards this aim. For instance, a possible solution might be the adoption of a management by projects solution. This approach could simultaneously increase employees' motivation and accountability, and the degree of organizational flexibility.

Chapter 3 explored dimensions such as individual behaviors, personal qualities, and interpersonal relationships in the public service environment, with a specific focus on the Italian setting. Questionnaires and interviews with 156 Italian public managers, officers, and employees allowed for the analysis of issues regarding job characteristics, leadership/managerial style, human resource management (personal motivation and incentives), organizational climate, individual targets, and public administration of affiliation targets. These issues are key points in answering the research questions and achieving the aim of understanding which organizational features characterize Italian public administration. The analysis was carried out through a correlation test and a linear regression.

Most of the participants (nearly 80%) are 40-50 years of age, they have mostly been in service for 10-20 years (44%), and come from local (48%) and central government (27%) institutions. Most of them are officers (56%), while 31% are employees, and 13% are managers.

Concerning the activities public servants carry out, findings show that both horizontal specialization and vertical specialization are "relatively high" (71% and 67%) or "high" (23% and 27%). Indeed, a "relatively high" motivation comes out among 40% of the participants, and "high" motivation among 19% of the participants. Asked what kind of solutions would improve employees' motivation in the public service, most participants gave greater importance to career development (42%) and monetary incentives (33%). Only 15% reported the development of informal leadership, 8% indicated non-monetary incentives, and just 2% recognized superiors adopting behaviors to set an example for their employees.

Results relating to the formalization degree show that the balance needle is more oriented toward a low degree (38% "relatively low"; 52% when cumulating "null", "low" and "relatively low"). There are nevertheless high percentages of "relatively high" (31%) and "high" (15%).

Results for the question "what do you think is the priority of your PA of affiliation?" interestingly show that the priority of the PA is represented in 68% of the cases by "respecting the rules." Asked for their personal targets, participants mostly reported "reaching PA targets" (35%), followed by "finding solutions to citizens' problems" (33%) and "respecting the rules" (29%). Indeed, "reaching individual targets" represented only 4%.

Another question asked participants to indicate which managerial style is mainly adopted within their PA of affiliation: anarchy resulted as the most selected style (33%), while the second choice was "coercive" (31%).

Finally, relating to the degree of conflict, more than half of the participants reported a "relatively high" (52%) degree of conflict, and another relevant percentage (29%) reported a "high" level of conflict.

The correlation test aimed at understanding which relationships might exist between age; degrees of conflict and horizontal vertical, and formalization specialization; personal motivation, job qualification; public administration of affiliation; public administration's priority; managerial styles; and solutions to improve motivation. The results also enabled the understanding of the features characterizing the different types of public administration. The test revealed that by examining the characteristics of the central government emerging from the analysis, the resulting model perfectly reflected NPM features (performance as the priority, high formalization degree, developed role for employees, and monetary incentives).

By examining the characteristics of the local government, the model mostly presented the characteristics of the classic bureaucracy (attention to rules, high horizontal and vertical specialization degree, low degree of motivation).

Health and social care institutions presented the characteristics of the professional bureaucracy model by showing a positive correlation with the orientation towards customer satisfaction and with career development as the main incentive to improve employees' motivation.

Indeed, public administrations in the education and research fields show positive correlations with the characteristics concerning anarchy, even though they also show a strong and positive correlation with high degrees of motivation.

Social insurance institutions proved to be the most informal type of public administration due to the positive correlation with the adoption of a participative managerial style, a high motivation degree, and a motivation incentive represented by the presence of informal leadership.

The linear regression was performed to test the dependence of personal motivation on the specialization degree, the complexity degree, the formalization degree, the conflict degree, and the managerial style. The analysis revealed that personal motivation has a positive relationship with high degrees of specialization (both horizontal and vertical), a high formalization degree, and a negative relationship with the degree of conflict, while no significant relationship emerges with the managerial style.

Participants were also asked to provide their own suggestions to improve their public administrations. With regard to the degree of horizontal job specialization, most participants (46%) had no suggestions, while 40% answered that there is a need to increase employees' job training. This result is interesting considering the high level of motivation associated with a high level of specialization; this may also be confirmed by the fact that other replies, despite amounting to only 4%, indicated the need to "increase specialization," as the respondents seemed to feel comforted by a high level of specialization.

Even in the case of interventions in the degree of vertical job specialization, most participants (60%) had no suggested solutions. The most important answer related to the vertical specialization degree, "increasing decisional autonomy," which only reached 8%. Answers that received more attention included "increasing collaboration" (12%) and "process re-engineering" (10%).

More than half of participants did not have solutions to reduce/improve the degree of formalization; and 27% mentioned interventions that involve a clearer attribution of roles and responsibilities.

Concerning the desired managerial style, most participants (88%) indicated a participative style, while 10% reported a democratic style and 2% asserted that "leadership is not required; only coercion and authority are needed."

Regarding interventions for conflict resolution, half of the participants indicated "sharing targets with employees" and 19% indicated "creating a positive organizational climate."

As for participants' solutions to resolve bureaucratic inefficiencies, interestingly 62% gave answers that can be labeled as "working on individual behaviors," while 29% proposed adopting organizational models based on project management. Among other answers, 4% of participants reported the need to reduce excessive regulations.

Finally, to verify which model occurs overall in the Italian public sector, Mintzberg's (1979) specialization matrix was applied to determine whether Weber's statement about the high specialization degree associated with the bureaucratic model also occurs in the specific case analyzed. On this basis tasks' characteristics (from participants' answers about their tasks' specialization degrees) were analyzed. The results show high degrees of specialization (both horizontal and vertical), thus confirming that the tasks performed by participants may be collocated perfectly within the bureaucratic domain. According to the literature, these kinds of tasks are usually associated with a low degree of motivation due to the high specialization and repetition of activities carried out by employees. Indeed, in the analyzed case public servants show a quite high degree of motivation that leads to the consideration of what was stated by Merton (1940) – that bureaucrats took pride in their craft and that this in turn leads them to resist changes in established routines.

The findings of the analysis reveal two faces of the Italian public sector. On one side, there are "happy bureaucrats," quite surprisingly strongly motivated by repetitive and standardized tasks, monetary incentives, and strongly motivated to maintain the status quo, as revealed by the high percentages of participants not reporting/proposing solutions to solve problems related to the degree of specialization and formalization. A related consideration might be the fact that the introduction of NPM principles has probably only led to employees' target transposition from rules to the achievement of personal targets related to monetary incentives.

On the other side, there is a worrying high percentage (33%) of participants reporting "anarchy" as the organizational model mainly adopted within their public administration, accompanied by no clear attribution of roles and responsibilities and no employee involvement (27%).

Results indicate that apparently in Italy the reform led by the NPM principles during the 1990s has never been completed. The NPM principles have only been applied partially to some aspects of the public service provision process, while managers and employees are still rooted in the ancient bureaucratic way of thinking, operating, and behaving. Moreover, they appear to be "happy" to be bureaucrats, despite being trapped in standardized and repetitive tasks. The NPM introduction of monetary incentives, related to the achievement of specific targets, seems to be a sufficient reward and motivating factor for Italian public servants.

On this basis, results show that a decoupling is taking place between theory and practice. While theory suggests that employees carrying out repetitive tasks suffer from turnover, alienation, and low motivation, in practice, at least in the case analyzed, employees show a high degree of motivation, as it seems that they are defending the status quo that allows "doing less for having more.".

Surely, the Italian government should consider reducing excessive regulations, which often create overlapping laws and confusing situations, for which public employees themselves have no instruments to find solutions.

Then, the fact that many participants spontaneously indicated "anarchy" as the "organizational model" operating in their administration shows that the Italian government needs to rethink the way in which public administrations are organized and managed, especially in consideration of the fact that 27% of the participants highlighted no clear attribution of roles and responsibilities within their administration.

Thus, the results from questionnaires and interviews confirm that the core problem in public administration is related to the lack of an organizational culture oriented toward the public interest, rather than the interest of managers and employees in attaining personal performance rewards. The second, related step is the recourse to a behavioral approach (Chapter 2), to ensure that managers' and employees' behaviors are in line with the development of a different culture that should then improve the way in which public administrations are managed and organized to pursue the public interest.

This book contributes to the debate on public administration.

First, it provides a complete, updated, and in-depth analysis of the main bureaucratic and post-bureaucratic issues by reviewing and discussing previous literature on the theme.

Second, it contributes to the claim that effective change in the public sector should consider focusing on individuals and their behaviors, by employing a different approach to study and manage public organizations. Individuals represent the core of organizations, and the way they behave and interact may shape and define the way in which the organization itself behaves and carries out its activities. This issue is of key importance especially in public administration, where the actions affect a multitude of stakeholders.

Third, the findings support the understanding of the changes in Italy and Southern Europe, which are often less considered within studies on the public sector. Findings from the systematic review highlighted a strong focus on Anglo-Saxon countries, while Southern European countries are less regarded.

Fourth, since the questionnaire faces crucial themes regarding the public sector, such as specialization, formalization, motivation, conflict, and managerial styles, it could be argued that this book has key implications for academics and practitioners. Also, it might represent a first step of a more in-depth analysis on the perception held by individuals working in the public sector of their own environment. This assessment, in turn, becomes crucial to individuate solutions to change those managerial practices and those individual behaviors still rooted in the old approach to bureaucracy, which might be unhealthy both for public administration and their stakeholders. In this regard, the discussion of these issues may support the development of solutions to improve operational management and perform better change management in the public sector: if the awareness about the above-mentioned dimensions is also raised in the public-sector domain, it will be possible to develop better organizational models that balance the satisfaction of public stakeholders and respect toward performance and efficiency.

In this way, this book provides concepts and empirical findings with implications useful for academics, public managers, and policy makers.

## References

Ahn M.J., and Bretschneider S. (2011), Politics of E-Government: E-Government and the Political Control of Bureaucracy, *Public Administration Review*, vol. 71, no. 3, pp. 414-424. doi: 10.1111/j.1540-6210.2011.02225.x.

Alexander D., Lewis J.M., and Considine M. (2011), How Politicians and Bureaucrats Network: A Comparison Across Governments, *Public Administration*, vol. 89, no. 4, pp. 1274-1292. doi: 10.1111/j.1467-9299.2010.01890.x.

Bang H.P. (2004), Culture Governance: Governing Self-Reflexive Modernity, *Public Administration*, vol. 82, no. 1, pp. 157-190, doi: 10.1111/j.0033-3298.2004.00389.x.

Berg A.M. (2006), Transforming public services – transforming the public servant?, *International Journal of Public Sector Management*, vol. 19, no. 6, pp. 556-568, doi: 10.1108/09513550610686627.

Blau P.M., (1955), *The dynamics of bureaucracy: a study of interpersonal relations in two Government Agencies*, Chicago: University of Chicago Press.

Bode I., and Dent M. (2014), Converging hybrid worlds? Medicine and hospital management in Europe, *International Journal of Public Sector Management*, vol. 27, no. 5, doi: 10.1108/IJPSM-01-2013-0011.

Callanan M. (2005), Institutionalizing Participation and Governance? New Participative Structures in Local Government in Ireland, *Public Administration*, vol. 83, no. 4, pp. 909-929. doi: 10.1111/j.0033-3298.2005.00483.x.

Carey G., and Matthews M. (2017), Methods for Delivering Complex Social Services: Exploring adaptive management and regulation in the Australian national disability insurance scheme, *Public Management Review*, vol. 19, no. 2, pp. 194-211, doi:10.1080/14719037.2016.1148194.

Charlesworth J., Clarke J., and Cochrane A. (1996), Tangled Webs? Managing Local Mixed Economies Of Care, *Public Administration*, vol. 74, no. 1, pp. 67-88, doi: 10.1111/j.1467-9299.1996.tb00858.x.

Cloutier C., Denis J.L., Langley A., and Lamothe L. (2016), Agency at the Managerial Interface: Public Sector Reform as Institutional Work, *Journal of Public Administration Research and Theory*, vol. 26, no. 2, pp. 259-276, doi: 10.1093/jopart/muv009.

Considine M. (2000), Contract Regimes and Reflexive Governance: Comparing Employment Service Reforms in the United Kingdom, the Netherlands, New Zealand and Australia, *Public Administration*, vol. 78, no. 3, pp. 613-638, doi: 10.1111/1467-9299.00221.

Correia, T., and Denis, J.L. (2016), Hybrid management, organizational configuration, and medical professionalism: evidence from the establishment of a clinical directorate in Portugal, *BMC Health Services Research*, vol. 16, SI 2, pp. 161-171, doi: 10.1186/s12913-016-1398-2.

Currie G., Grubnic S., and Hodges R. (2011), Leadership In Public Services Networks: Antecedents, Process And Outcome, *Public Administration*, vol. 89, no. 2, pp. 242-264, doi: 10.1111/J.1467-9299.2011.01931.X.

Currie, G., and Procter, S.J. (2005), The antecedents of middle managers' strategic contribution: The case of a professional bureaucracy, *Journal Of Management Studies*, vol. 42, no. 7, pp. 1325-1356, doi: 10.1111/j.1467-6486.2005.00546.x.

De Boer H.F., Enders J., and Leisyte L. (2007), Public Sector Reform In Dutch Higher Education: The Organizational Transformation Of The University, *Public Administration*, vol. 85, no. 1, pp. 27-46, doi: 10.1111/j.1467-9299.2007.00632.x.

Entwistle T., and Martin S. (2005), From Competition to Collaboration in Public Service Delivery: A New Agenda for Research, *Public Administration*, vol. 83, no. 1, pp. 233-242, doi: 10.1111/j.0033-3298.2005.00446.x.

Finn, R., Currie, G., and Martin G. (2010), Team Work in Context: Institutional Mediation in the Public-service Professional Bureaucracy, *Organization Studies*, vol. 31, no. 8, pp. 1069-1097, doi: 10.1177/0170840610376142.

Fotaki M. (2011), Towards Developing New Partnerships In Public Services: Users As Consumers, Citizens And/Or Co-Producers In Health And Social Care In England And Sweden, *Public Administration*, vol. 89, no. 3, pp. 933-955, doi: 10.1111/j.1467-9299.2010.01879.x.

Gatenby M., Rees C., Truss C., Alfes K., and Soane E. (2015), Managing Change, or Changing Managers? The role of middle managers in UK public service reform, *Public Management Review*, vol. 17, no. 8, pp. 1124-1145, doi: 10.1080/1471 9037.2014.895028.

Geddes L., (2012), In Search of Collaborative Public Management, *Public Management Review*, vol. 14, no. 7, pp. 947-966, doi: 10.1080/14719037.2011.650057.

Germov, J. (2005), Managerialism in the Australian public health sector: towards the hyper-rationalisation of professional bureaucracies, *Sociology Of Health & Illness*, vol. 27, no. 6, pp. 738-758, doi: 10.1111/j.1467-9566.2005.00472.x.

Gourdin, G., and Schepers, R. (2009), Hospital governance and the medical practitioner in Belgium, *Journal Of Health Organization And Management*, vol. 23, no. 3, pp. 319-331, doi: 10.1108/14777260910966744.

Hammerschmid G., and Meyer R.E. (2005), New Public Management in Austria: Local Variation on a Global Theme?, *Public Administration*, vol. 83, no. 3, pp. 709-733, doi: 10.1111/j.0033-3298.2005.00471.x.

Hinna A., Mameli S., Mangia G. (2016), *La pubblica amministrazione in movimento. Competenze, comportamenti e regole*, Milano: Egea.

Hood C. (1991), A Public Management for all Seasons?, *Public Administration*, vol. 69, no. 1, pp. 3-39. doi: 10.1111/j.1467-9299.1991.tb00778.x.

Huse, M. (2007), *Boards, Governance and Value Creation*, Cambridge: Cambridge University Press.

Jeffares S., and Skelcher C. (2011), Democratic Subjectivities In Network Governance: A Q Methodology Study Of English And Dutch Public Managers, *Public Administration*, vol. 89, no. 4, pp. 1253-1273, doi: 10.1111/j.1467-9299.2010.01888.x.

Kane J., and Patapan H. (2006), In Search of Prudence: The Hidden Problem of Managerial Reform, *Public Administration Review*, vol. 66, no. 5, pp. 711-724, doi: 10.1111/j.1540-6210.2006.00636.x.

Kelly J. (2006), Central Regulation Of English Local Authorities: An Example Of Meta-Governance?, *Public Administration*, vol. 84, no. 3, pp. 603-621, doi: 10.1111/j.1467-9299.2006.00604.x.

Kickert W.J.M. (2005), Distinctiveness in the study of public management in Europe, *Public Management Review*, vol. 7, no. 4, pp. 537-563, doi: 10.1080/1471 9030500362470.

Kickert W.J.M. (2011), Distinctiveness Of Administrative Reform In Greece, Italy, Portugal And Spain. Common Characteristics Of Context, Administrations And Reforms, *Public Administration*, vol. 89, no. 3, pp. 801-818, doi: 10.1111/j.1467-9299.2010.01862.x.

Kinder T. (2012), Learning, Innovating and Performance in Post-New Public Management of Locally Delivered Public Services, *Public Management Review*, vol. 14, no. 3, pp. 403-428, doi: 10.1080/14719037.2011.637408.

Kirkpatrick I. (1999), Managers or Colleagues?, *Public Management: An International Journal of Research and Theory*, vol. 1, no. 4, pp. 489-509, doi: 10.1080/1471903 9900000023.

Kirkpatrick I., and Ackroyd S. (2003), Transforming the professional archetype?, *Public Management Review*, vol. 5, no. 4, pp. 509-529. doi: 10.1080/1471903032000178563.

Kitchener M., and Gask L. (2003), NPM merger mania. Lessons from an early case, *Public Management Review*, vol. 5, no. 1, pp. 19-44. doi: 10.1080/1461667022000028843.

Klijn, E.H. (2008), Complexity theory and Public Administration: what's new? Key concepts in complexity theory compared to their counterparts in public administration, *Public Management Review*, vol. 10, n. 3, pp. 299-317. doi: 10.1080/147 19030802002675

Knott J.H., Miller G.J. (2006), Social welfare, corruption and credibility, *Public Management Review*, vol. 8, no. 2, pp. 227-252, doi: 10.1080/14719030600587455.

Knott J. H. (2011), Federalist No. 10: Are Factions the Problem in Creating Democratic Accountability in the Public Interest?, *Public Administration Review*, vol. 71, SI 1, pp. s29-s36, doi: 10.1111/j.1540-6210.2011.02459.x.

Kooiman J., Jentoft S. (2009), Meta-governance: values, norms and principles, and the making of hard choices, *Public Administration*, vol. 87, no. 4, pp. 818-836. doi: 10.1111/j.1467-9299.2009.01780.x.

Kothari, S., and Handscombe, R. D. (2007), Sweep or seep? Structure, culture, enterprise and universities, *Management Decision*, vol. 45, no. 1, pp. 43-61, doi: 10.1108/00251740710718953.

Lapsley I. (2008), The NPM Agenda: back to the future, *Financial Accountability & Management*, vol. 24, no. 1, pp. 77-96. doi: 10.1111/j.1468-0408.2008.00444.x.

Lapsley I. (2009), New Public Management: The Cruellest Invention of the Human Spirit?, *ABACUS*, vol. 45, no. 1, pp. 1-21. doi: 10.1111/j.1467-6281.2009.00275.x.

Learmonth M. (2005), Doing Things with Words: The Case of 'Management' and 'Administration', *Public Administration*, vol. 83, no. 3, pp. 617-637, doi: 10.1111/j.0033-3298.2005.00465.x.

Lega, F., and DePietro, C. (2005), Converging patterns in hospital organization: beyond the professional bureaucracy, *Health Policy*, vol. 74, no. 3, pp. 261-281, doi: 10.1016/j.healthpol.2005.01.010.

Magone J.M. (2011), The Difficult Transformation Of State And Public Administration In Portugal. Europeanization And The Persistence Of Neo-Patrimonialism, *Public Administration*, vol. 89, no. 3, pp. 756-782, doi: 10.1111/j.1467-9299.2011.01913.x.

Martin G.P. (2011), The Third Sector, User Involvement And Public Service Reform: A Case Study In The Co-Governance Of Health Service Provision, *Public Administration*, vol. 89, no. 3, pp. 909-932, doi: 10.1111/j.1467-9299.2011.01910.x.

Martin G.P., Currie G., and Finn R. (2009), Leadership, Service Reform, and Public-Service Networks: The Case of Cancer-Genetics Pilots in the English NHS, *Jour-*

*nal of Public Administration Research and Theory*, vol. 19, no. 4, pp. 769-794, doi:10.1093/jopart/mun016.

McClelland D.C., (1961), *The Achieving Society*. New York: Free Press.

McGivern G., Currie G., Ferlie E., Fitzgerald L., and Waring J. (2015), Hybrid Manager-Professionals' Identity Work: The Maintenance And Hybridization Of Medical Professionalism In Managerial Contexts, *Public Administration*, vol. 93, no. 2, pp. 412-432, doi: 10.1111/padm.12119.

Meek J.W., (2010), Complexity Theory for Public Administration and Policy, *Emergence: Complexity & Organization*, vol. 12, n. 1, pp. 1-4.

Meier K.J., and Bohte J. (2001), Structure and Discretion: Missing Links in Representative Bureaucracy, *Journal of Public Administration Research and Theory*, vol. 11, no. 4, pp. 455-470, doi: 10.1093/oxfordjournals.jpart.a003511.

Merton R.K., (1940), Bureaucratic Structure and Personality, *Social Forces*, vol. 18, n. 4, pp. 560-568. doi: 10.2307/2570634.

Meyer R.E., Egger-Peitler I., Höllerer M.A., Hammerschmid G. (2014), Of Bureaucrats And Passionate Public Managers: Institutional Logics, Executive Identities, And Public Service Motivation, *Public Administration*, vol. 92, no. 4, pp. 861-885, doi: 10.1111/j.1467-9299.2012.02105.x.

Meynhardt T., and Diefenbach F.E. (2012), What Drives Entrepreneurial Orientation in the Public Sector? Evidence from Germany's Federal Labor Agency, *Journal of Public Administration Research and Theory*, vol. 22, no. 4, pp. 761-792, doi:10.1093/jopart/mus013.

Mintzberg, H. (1979), *The Structuring of Organizations*, Englewood Cliffs: Prentice Hall.

Nielsen V.L. (2006), Are Street-Level Bureaucrats Compelled Or Enticed To Cope?, *Public Administration*, vol. 84, no. 4, pp. 861-889, doi: 10.1111/j.1467-9299.2006.006 16.x.

Noordegraaf M., and Abma T. (2003), Management by Measurement? Public Management Practices Amidst Ambiguity, *Public Administration*, vol. 81, no. 4, pp. 853-871, doi: 10.1111/j.0033-3298.2003.00374.x.

Noordegraaf M., and De Wit B. (2012), Responses To Managerialism: How Management Pressures Affect Managerial Relations And Loyalties In Education, *Public Administration*, vol. 90, no. 4, pp. 957-973, doi: 10.1111/j.1467-9299.2012.02068.x.

Ongaro E. (2006), The Dynamics Of Devolution Processes In Legalistic Countries: Organizational Change In The Italian Public Sector, *Public Administration*, vol. 84, no. 3, pp. 737-770, doi: 10.1111/j.1467-9299.2006.00610.x.

Orr K., and Vince R. (2009), Traditions Of Local Government, *Public Administration*, vol. 87, no. 3, pp. 655-677, doi: 10.1111/j.1467-9299.2009.01770.x.

Osborne S.P. (2010a), "The (New) Public Governance: a suitable case for treatment", Chap. 1 in *The New Public Governance?* London: Routledge.

Osborne S.P. (2010b), "Public governance and public service delivery: a research agenda for the future", Chap. 23 in *The New Public Governance?* London: Routledge.

Pollitt C. (2009), Bureaucracies Remember, Post-Bureaucratic Organizations Forget?, *Public Administration*, vol. 87, no. 2, pp. 198-218, doi: 10.1111/J.1467-9299.2008.01738.X

Pollitt, C., and Bouckaert, G. (2000), *Public management reform: An international comparison*, Oxford: Oxford University Press.

Power M., (1999), *The Audit Society*, Oxford: Oxford University Press.

Raadschelders J.C.N. (1995), Rediscovering Citizenship: Historical And Contemporary Reflections, *Public Administration*, vol. 73, no. 4, pp. 611-625. doi: 10.1111/j.1467-9299.1995.tb00849.x.

Rothstein, H., Downer, J. (2012), 'Renewing Defra': Exploring the emergence of risk-based policymaking in UK central government, *Public Administration*, vol. 90, pp. 781-799. doi:10.1111/j.1467-9299.2011.01999.x.

Seibel W. (2010), Beyond Bureaucracy – Public Administration as Political Integrator and Non-Weberian Thought in Germany, *Public Administration Review*, vol. 70, no. 5, pp. 719-730, doi: 10.1111/j.1540-6210.2010.02200.x.

Simon H. (1956), Rational choice and the structure of the environment, *Psychological Review*, vol. 63, no. 2, pp. 129-138. Doi: 10.1037/h0042769.

Tichelar, M. (1997), Professional bureaucracy as a barrier to management learning in the public services: A personal reflection, *Local Government Studies*, vol. 23, no. 2, pp. 14-25. doi: 10.1080/03003939708433862.

Vinot D. (2014), Transforming hospital management à la francaise: The new role of clinical managers in French public hospitals, *International Journal of Public Sector Management*, vol. 27 (5): pp. 406-416, doi: 10.1108/IJPSM-06-2012-0067.

Voets J., Verhoest K., and Molenveld A. (2015), Coordinating for Integrated Youth Care: The need for smart metagovernance, *Public Management Review*, vol. 17, no. 7, pp. 981-1001, doi: 10.1080/14719037.2015.1029347.

Weber M., (1922), *Economy and Society*, Berkeley: University of California Press.

Williams B.N., Kang S.-C., and Johnson J. (2016), (Co)-Contamination as the Dark Side of Co-Production: Public value failures in co-production processes, *Public Management Review*, vol. 18, no. 5, pp. 692-717, doi: 10.1080/14719037.2015.1111660.

For Product Safety Concerns and Information please contact our EU
representative  GPSR@taylorandfrancis.com
Taylor & Francis Verlag GmbH, Kaufingerstraße 24, 80331 München, Germany

www.ingramcontent.com/pod-product-compliance
Ingram Content Group UK Ltd.
Pitfield, Milton Keynes, MK11 3LW, UK
UKHW020946180425
457613UK00019B/548